HAYLEY WESTENRA

The World at Her Feet

Paul Little

PENGUIN BOOKS

PENGUIN BOOKS

Published by the Penguin Group

Penguin Group (NZ), cnr Airborne and Rosedale Roads, Albany,
Auckland 1310, New Zealand (a division of Pearson New Zealand Ltd)
Penguin Group (USA) Inc., 375 Hudson Street,
New York, New York 10014, USA
Penguin Group (Canada), 10 Alcorn Avenue, Toronto,
Ontario, Canada M4V 3B2 (a division of Pearson Penguin Canada Inc.)
Penguin Books Ltd, 80 Strand, London, WC2R 0RL, England
Penguin Ireland, 25 St Stephen's Green,
Dublin 2, Ireland (a division of Penguin Books Ltd)
Penguin Group (Australia), 250 Camberwell Road, Camberwell,
Victoria 3124, Australia (a division of Pearson Australia Group Pty Ltd)
Penguin Books India Pvt Ltd, 11, Community Centre,
Panchsheel Park, New Delhi - 110 017, India
Penguin Books (South Africa) (Pty) Ltd, 24 Sturdee Avenue,
Rosebank, Johannesburg 2196, South Africa

Penguin Books Ltd, Registered Offices: 80 Strand, London, WC2R 0RL, England

First published by Penguin Group (NZ), 2004
1 3 5 7 9 10 8 6 4 2

Designed and Typeset by Egan-Reid Ltd, Auckland
Printed in Australia by McPherson's Printing Group

ISBN 0 14 301926 0
A catalogue record for this book is available
from the National Library of New Zealand.

www.penguin.co.nz

Contents

Prologue

Nobody told Hayley Westenra that Sir Andrew Lloyd Webber wanted her to sing for the Queen until the last possible minute. She was in Tokyo in late 2003, with her manager Steve Abbott and father Gerald, promoting her record- and ground-breaking album *Pure*. Her agent received an email from Lloyd Webber's Really Useful Group (RUG) saying Hayley was wanted to sing at a private function. Would she be interested?

At this stage the RUG people were not letting on that this was a rather exclusive private function. The audience would include, as well as the Queen, UK Prime Minister Tony Blair and US President George W. Bush. Within Hayley's immediate circle this trio would be abbreviated eventually to BBQ or 'barbeque'.

Hayley was a long-time Lloyd Webber fan, having included songs by him on two of her four albums to date. Her mother Jill had videotaped the composer's fiftieth birthday party and many of his other shows for the family to enjoy. When Hayley was eleven and much of her performing consisted of busking for audiences of shoppers in Christchurch malls, Jill had bought, at her daughter's request, a book of his songs to pick material from.

Yes, Hayley was interested.

Steve Abbott contacted the Really Useful Group for details of the audition. 'I said, "Is she going to meet Andrew?" They said, "We don't know. There will be one of his people there." I thought fair enough. There's no way any kind of musician can get in close quarters with Hayley and not be blown away.'

After that, events moved quickly. Back in London, Gerald got a call from Steve saying Hayley was expected the following evening at the RUG headquarters, not far from her flat in Covent Garden. He decided not to tell Hayley because he was worried she would stress and not sleep well that night.

The next morning, Hayley says, 'I had just woken up and Dad was saying, "Sir Andrew Lloyd Webber's organising this gig." He went on about it for a while, then he said, "You've got an audition with him tonight." And I was, "Oh gosh."'

According to Gerald, Hayley was a little more than 'Oh gosh'. 'She told me off for telling her so late,' says Gerald, 'but I had a good reason.'

Gerald had made the right decision. Although others would not have noticed, those close to Hayley could tell she was uncharacteristically nervous when she arrived at Lloyd Webber's headquarters later that day. But her gift for keeping herself calm in situations that could well faze any other performer got her through.

'I went into this room like a conservatory, with a grand piano,' says Hayley. 'At first there was just the musical director. He gave me the music and said, "We'll go through it before *he* comes." It was good having the extra time to go over it. I was doing this song called "I Believe My Heart" from *The Woman in White*, his new musical. Then I heard this creak behind me and thought, Oh my gosh! I knew it was him. I carried on. Then the piano stopped. Sir Andrew shook my hand and said, "It sounds great."

'He was really warm and made me feel at ease. Then he said, "We'll have to find another piece for you to sing, but it has to be one of mine." I suggested "Wishing You Were Somehow Here Again" from *Phantom of the Opera*. And he said, "Very well, I'll play." So he was playing and I was singing, praying I wouldn't forget the words. I'd sung it a long time ago, when I was like eleven. I wasn't nervous singing that. But the whole time I was thinking, This is weird. It's Andrew Lloyd Webber on the piano and I'm singing. It'd all happened so fast.

'In the end, we went for "Pie Jesu" from his *Requiem*, because it's more of a classic Andrew Lloyd Webber piece.' The composer told the young singer she would be guaranteed to wow the audience with his showstopper. 'Then we started from the beginning and went through everything again. At the end he said, "Everything they've said about you is true. You've got the job."'

Outside, Steve had been waiting with Gerald. 'I've seen Hayley nervous but never visibly nervous like she was then,' he says. 'We could hear her in the reception. "Pie Jesu" was going on in the background. Then she went into more of the

Andrew Lloyd Webber repertoire. She just knocked them out one after the other, word perfect. It sounded exhilarating.'

Eventually Hayley emerged.

'How'd it go?' asked Steve.

'Good,' said Hayley. 'Halfway through his eyes got all moist.'

Steve followed up the next day with Lloyd Webber's people, still not letting on that he knew who Hayley would be singing for. 'They said, "We really like her and we have this thing – the Queen thing. Would Hayley like to be part of it?"'

Steve had some reservations about the political implications of his apolitical teenage performer singing for the US leader in a context of the war in Iraq. 'I had buzzing round all the negative possibilities with Bush. Hayley shouldn't be political at the moment.' In the end he decided that if it was okay with the Queen, it was going to be okay with Hayley.

The concert was the following week and, for security reasons, arrangements were left to the last minute, leaving little time for anything to go awry. Details were kept to a minimum. By now Jill had flown in from New Zealand to take over Hayley duties from Gerald. 'We were reassured it was definitely happening,' says Steve. 'But no one was being told anything.'

While security checks were being run on Hayley, she was sent the music to learn. She was still doing so the day before the performance. In combination with two Lloyd Webber protégés she was to sing four numbers: 'Pie Jesu' as a solo, 'I Believe My Heart' with Kevin McKidd, a portion of 'Let Us Love in Peace' with Shonagh Daly, and 'No Matter What' for the finale with the other artists.

'On the day, we went down to the rehearsal only three hours

before she did it,' recalls Steve. 'It was the first time she got to sing the duet. Hayley just got up in the rehearsal room and did it. Everyone, including the pianist, was like "Wow!"'

Lloyd Webber called in on the rehearsal. Steve noted that the composer couldn't take his eyes off the young New Zealander. 'He was clearly fixated.'

'We had some sandwiches, then had to get changed,' says Hayley. 'Then everyone else left, and it was just the artists and the musical director. Sir Andrew went early to go to the dinner. We all went in this van with blacked-out windows, through about six barricades to get to the venue, which was the American ambassador's residence.' There were police checks, FBI checks, checks Hayley didn't even realise were happening.

'A lot of the time they would just count the number of people and check there was nothing suspicious,' says Hayley. 'But the funny thing was, when we got to the venue they spent ages searching my bag. I'd just chucked everything in. It was amazing that everything had to be checked, despite the fact that it had already been X-rayed.'

Winfield House, in London's Regent's Park, is a magnificent red-brick Georgian-style mansion, built in the 1930s by Woolworths heiress Barbara Hutton and donated by her to the US government to be used as the ambassador's home. The artists arrived at the venue half an hour before the performance was due to start and were herded into a cloakroom to wait. While the BBQ troika, along with some sixty other guests, including Prince Charles, Colin Powell, Condoleeza Rice, Cherie Blair and Laura Bush, finished their meals, Hayley used the time to go over and over the words in her head. The artists were issued with lyric sheets, just in case. 'The scary thing was that, just when I was about to go on for my duet, there was one word I couldn't remember, so I had to grab my sheet to remind me. I was in a huge fluster, then I had to walk out to sing, acting completely composed. I was really nervous, but pulled myself together enough to get through it.'

Winfield House is famously well appointed. Although the room was small, just big enough to contain the tables at which the guests sat, it was dominated by an enormous chandelier and magnificent paintings.

'I was brushing up against the people at the tables when I was singing,' recalls Hayley. 'I had a choice of whether to look directly ahead or at the sides. I thought, I better compose myself and not look around, but at the same time I was scanning the room. It was weird, because I saw George Bush with a smile on his face, leaning back in his chair to get a better view. And the Queen there, sitting a bit more upright.'

At the end there was a receiving line with handshakes, photos and compliments.

'They all went, "Well done, that was great." I remember Bush saying, "It really capped off the evening. You've got a fantastic voice."'

Hayley caught up briefly with one old acquaintance. 'Prince Charles came past and I went, "Oh you came to my primary school when I was six." He said, "Did I?" I said, "It's all right, you don't have to remember."'

It was already a late night, but after the performance Lloyd Webber took his artists to supper. Keen as ever to maximise exposure for his charge, Steve Abbott had alerted TVNZ's

London correspondent, Ian Sinclair, who waited with him in the cold outside the restaurant for the party to arrive. 'We waited for about an hour and a half to make sure she got there safely,' says Steve, 'but also to get the story. They did an interview. She was so excited. I'd already contacted the show's producer who had said she was absolutely fantastic.'

And the evening's excitement wasn't over yet. 'Just as I was about to leave,' says Hayley, 'Andrew Lloyd Webber came up and said, "Well done, you were great." And he offered to write me a song. "I'd love to write a song for you, if you'd like me to." And I was like, "Are you kidding?"'

At sixteen, Hayley Westenra had come a very long way in a very short time. And it was all thanks to a remarkable group of people, not least of them her parents.

CHAPTER ONE

The Littlest Star

Indirectly, it was music that brought Hayley's parents together. Jill Ireland had moved to Christchurch to study for an arts degree. On her first night in town, she and a friend were invited to the after-show party for *Anno Domini*, a now-forgotten musical in which Gerald Westenra had been a performer. While looking for the party, Jill had noticed 'a cute guy' through the window of a house. Further enquiries revealed it to be the location of the party. Jill and her friend went in. Jill sat down next to an empty seat which was soon claimed by the cute guy, Gerald Westenra, a car parts salesman.

The name Westenra is Dutch. Gerald's antecedents came to New Zealand via Ireland (where there is still a crumbling castle in the family's name), and settled in Canterbury in the mid-nineteenth century. His father, Aylmer, was a pilot and farmer who contracted polio before Gerald was born. Later confined to a wheelchair, he owned a library and died when Gerald was fourteen. Patricia, Gerald's mother, was a nurse.

Jill Ireland grew up on the West Coast where her parents, Shirley and Gerry, had a bed-and-breakfast house. Gerry also drove tankers for Dominion Breweries.

Gerald helped Jill find a flat and the two started seeing each other. Before he left on a long-planned OE they became engaged. But instead of the anticipated minimum of six months, it was only a matter of days before Gerald found himself missing Jill too much and returned to Christchurch. The two moved in together and were married within the year.

Jill, whose final school report had said she would be able to do anything she put her mind to, was restless. She had given up, dissatisfied, on university, gone to work for a building society and tried agricultural college, all within a few short years.

'I was concerned I'd be stuck in an office all my life,' says Jill. 'I had a half day every month that was free, so I went to a school and helped a friend in her classroom. I thought, This feels good – maybe I can do teaching. I went off to teachers' college, and then I got pregnant. I remember Gerald, who got the call about the results when I was at college, ringing up and saying, "You're going to be a mum."'

Jill Westenra is a woman who does nothing by halves. It is one of the reasons she tried so many careers as a young adult: if she could not find the enthusiasm to devote herself totally to an occupation, there was no point doing it half-pie. It was the same with pregnancy. She studied health writer Adele Davis in depth, drank herbal teas, and ate lamb's fry and salads for extra nutrients. She was determined to have the healthiest baby possible. Teachers' college provided plenty of ideas she would be able to put into practice with her own child, including those of alternative educationalist Glen Doman.

Hayley Dee Westenra arrived in perfect health on 10 April 1987. The name was the result of lots of thinking on long walks and, of course, of prodigious research as Jill hunted through books for possible names. Even then, it wasn't till Hayley was safely with them that her parents decided that would be her name. Hayley means 'hero' and comes from the heroine of a story in the girls' weekly *Tammy* which Jill read as a child. Dee was the name of a doll she used to own.

And classical music was played to Hayley – before and after birth – not because her mother had a premonition she might one day become an international singing star, but because her research told her it was good for babies' brain development.

'When I was pregnant, I read all the pregnancy books from all the libraries around Christchurch. When I finished with the town one, I moved on to the suburbs. I read about nutrition. I just wanted to do the best I could.' She was, she says, 'bored by the end of my pregnancy, so I read about everything you could do to make sure labour was as fast and painless as possible. Which it was.'

Jill did anything and everything to foster Hayley's development. In accord with the Doman canon, objects around the house were labelled with name cards to encourage early reading. When Hayley, who her mother remembers as a 'sort of "skinny-chubby" baby with little wobbly legs', could walk, if the pair were going to the local shops and Hayley wanted to get out of her pushchair and push it herself, then push it herself she did. Shopping trips were lengthy affairs. Everything was designed to include Hayley – 'which does make it hard work,' Jill admits. 'But they were the most natural thing to put in place all these ideas I had. I had a folder of notes from all the books I'd read.'

When Jill found out that babies like symmetry, she hand-made cards with bright symmetrical faces on them to stimulate Hayley. There were garish mobiles galore in her room.

'Someone from playgroup was here once and went to put her baby down in Hayley's room and said, "How does she ever get to sleep?" She slept fine but she didn't sleep through the night for the first two years. We tried leaving her, but it was too heart-wrenching.'

In later years, too, Jill says, 'I had trouble leaving my children [with other people]. They didn't like being left. Which is hardly surprising – they were having so much fun.'

Jill had finally found the creative outlet she had been searching for through her various careers and studies. 'My whole approach in life was that whatever I did I was intense about. School was where I got positive feedback and started to feel I could do things. I had a good relationship with teachers and didn't want to let them down.'

Hayley did many things early. 'She walked early,' Jill recalls, 'but we probably gave her opportunities to walk. She'd push a wooden trolley a friend made and we put bricks in it to slow her down.' This was the pattern that would be followed throughout Hayley's life. Her parents would provide her with opportunities, and she would make the most of them.

It was the same with singing as it was with dancing, acting and all the other activities in which Hayley showed an interest. It was also the same for her younger sister and brother when they arrived in their turn.

Jill and Gerald had decided to add to their family. Hayley's sister Sophie was born on 29 June 1990. Three years later a son, Isaac, was born on 9 June 1993.

All three children received the same amount of love and encouragement from their parents, 'which is why,' says Jill, 'I didn't want four – because we couldn't keep up.'

Jill and Gerald were determined to give all their children 'a really full childhood where they had everything: trips to the beach, to the mountains, seeing as much as possible of the countryside, experiencing as much as they could, going on boats and trains. We couldn't afford to go to tropical islands, but we did the TranzAlpine Express. New Zealand is a good place to give a full, rich childhood.'

Unusually, the Westenra children have only known one home, a house their parents bought in the Christchurch sub-urb of Fendalton when Jill was expecting Hayley. Fendalton, with its deserted footpaths and assertive stone homes, is a part of town that might be described as toffee-nosed, although that's a label that could never be applied to the Westenras.

Their house lies at the end of a long right-of-way, in a location chosen because Jill wanted to bring her children up away from traffic pollution. It also had a garden with enough room for yet more stimulation. It soon came to contain a hut, a tree house, a jungle gym, a rope swing (which has now grown into the tree from which it hangs) and a playhouse.

'I wanted them to have a magical childhood,' says Jill. 'So Hayley has had all that, and I think it's been quite a normal upbringing and it's really helped her. I think it does help adults to have had a good childhood.' Her own mother had lived through the Depression and gone out to work when Jill was small so that she could have little extras. Jill got a magazine once a week, or a chocolate bar if her mother went to the supermarket. Jill, in her turn, was keen that her own children have the same happy memories of their childhood that she had of hers.

Although the house is too small for three nearly grown children, there are no thoughts of moving. 'We're all attached to it, and have wonderful memories of it. I had this instinctive feeling that's important. Having that much security makes a kid able to go out and do the things Hayley's done.'

Hayley was, fortunately, a child who loved to do things. There were boxes of materials to use creatively, though not all of her young friends knew what to make of them. Jill remembers 'when she was three and had a friend here making cards. Her friend obviously hadn't made Christmas cards before and Hayley said, "Say something Christmassy and my mother will write it." She had to explain to her what to do.'

When the time came to start (organised) preschool education, Jill investigated all the local preschool facilities, and even visited ones the family couldn't afford, to see if they offered anything special. In the end she concluded that it would be best to go to a local centre because of the sense of community it would provide.

Hayley rewarded her mother's efforts with the placid temperament she has kept to this day. 'I don't think she's ever thrown a temper tantrum in her life,' says Jill.

Gerald Westenra says he and Jill never sat down and agreed on a philosophy of parenting. Their style just evolved out of their complementary natures. 'It's my nature to be a giving sort of person,' says Gerald, 'and Jill's nature is to do the best she can of any job. My children are first and foremost in my life.' Jill concedes that she sometimes found herself on the receiving end of 'negative comments about how I was doing things because it wasn't conventional. I was always defending it because I believed in it.' And she has had to continue to defend herself against criticism of her parenting. In later years, however, she has had no greater champion than her elder daughter.

Gerald had long left car parts behind to work as a gemologist. Having spent some time employed by a large chain, he decided to go out on his own when he discovered his job was taking hours away from his family. As his own boss he could ensure at least weekends free. While Gerald earned the living, Jill kept track of the music lessons and sports activities.

And there was a lot of music, right from the start. Gerald's mother was a fine singer, and both Jill's parents were gifted musically. Her mother, Shirley Ireland, though untrained, had a good voice with a large range and played the lead in local productions. Her father, also Gerald, but known as Gerry, could not read music but could play anything from the harmonica to the violin by ear. Jill remembers many weekends when her parents would play impromptu sessions in the local hotels. Family members say Hayley's voice is eerily reminiscent of her maternal grandmother's.

As Jill remembers it, her parents' abilities were unfulfilled because 'they come from that background where it's big-headed to put yourself forward to perform, and they were never big-headed.' Jill herself can sing, harmonised with her sister as a child, and would have loved to get up on stage, but recognised she did not have what it takes to become a performer. She became determined the sort of modesty that held her parents back would not hinder Hayley.

Jill and Gerald could have gagged her and chained her to a rock, and Hayley would have kept on singing. Her first documented performance was at the age of two and a half, when she was flower girl at the wedding of Jill's sister, Carol. Jill, who was matron of honour, didn't hear a thing. Carol did, and frequently had to suppress giggles.

'The story goes that she sang "Silent Night" right through, just quietly,' says Jill. 'She probably did go around singing as a toddler, but that's just what children do. I didn't think she might be a singer.'

Shirley Ireland treasures a tape of Hayley singing nursery rhymes, accompanied by Gerry Ireland on various instruments. But again it's the sort of thing many grandparents have and not necessarily a sign of greatness to come.

Other aspects of Hayley's character that would stand her in good stead for her future career were also apparent at an early age. A friend of Jill's with a child the same age as Hayley remembers 'a video of her at kindergarten. Everyone is running around and Hayley is painting. They're all screaming, and she's completely focused on her picture. Then she stops and looks around and absorbs what they're doing and goes back to her painting.'

'She's always been a very considerate child,' says another friend. 'At birthday parties she was always a bit motherly. She'd watch to see that everyone else was enjoying themselves.'

Opportunities to advance Hayley's development were taken as they arose. Hayley was learning to swim at two, and it was at the pool that Jill met lifelong friend Martine Carter, whose daughter, Emma, is still one of Hayley's best friends. On one occasion Jill was reading aloud from a letter which mentioned someone learning ballet. 'And Hayley said, "Mum, can I learn ballet when I'm four?" As far as I knew, she wouldn't have known what ballet was, but I found a shop that sold ballet things and they told me there were lessons in a church around the corner. So she started ballet at four.'

Naturally, when Hayley turned five and had to start primary school, Jill and Gerald considered all the options. They settled on nearby Fendalton Primary School because its proximity would make it easier for them to support activities, and because Hayley would be likely to make friends who lived nearby.

'I'll always remember Gerald and Jill at the first picnic at the beginning of the school year,' says one of Hayley's first teachers, Dawn Lavender. 'Hayley was the first of theirs at school and they were so interested in what was going on. They weren't pushy, just asking questions to get more knowledge. It was all about doing the best for Hayley.'

Being located in a salubrious area, Fendalton Primary tended to have pupils whose parents took an interest, who would deliver their children each morning and collect them each afternoon. In general, it was a level of involvement which made the teachers' jobs easier.

Its principal, Dale Hadley, believed in the value of music for young children, so provided plenty of opportunities for musical talent to out. As well as school music lessons, Hayley followed her natural bent into learning the recorder and violin at school, and piano outside school hours.

'As they got older, the junior school would have a whole-school assembly every two weeks,' says Lavender. 'Hayley would be in the school orchestra every time, playing violin. Then, when it was time for the choir to perform, she'd put her instrument down and get up on the stage and sing. She always participated.'

And not just in music. 'The school was also supportive of sport,' says Lavender. 'Hayley seemed to fit into everything. I can remember a cross-country race one time, seeing this little waif with these great big eyes, doing her best. She was just one of the kids. And she still comes across like that. But there's been a lot of hard work. Even in those days she'd be learning violin or flute and have classes before school.'

The musical highlight of the school calendar was the junior concert at the end of the year. All the performances were well attended by supportive parents and grandparents. When she was six, Hayley came home from school one day and told her mother she would need to take her ballet gear to school for the Christmas production. So Jill tucked it into her bag the next day. 'It didn't sound like a major,' says Jill. 'Of course, we were totally oblivious to what was happening at school. Hayley was a child of few words. She never came home and told me heaps. It was like getting blood out of a stone.'

(Like a lot of children, Hayley kept different parts of her personality for different occasions. Jill was once surprised to get a school report that mentioned Hayley's wonderful sense of humour. Her Hayley?)

Jill may not have thought her daughter's voice was anything particularly special at that age, but one of Hayley's teachers, Lesley Compton, who would have been exposed to a wider range of six-year-old abilities than Jill, recognised something special in the little girl. She gave Hayley a solo part. School philosophy was to give all its little stars a chance to shine, but Hayley's ability was so out of the ordinary an exception was sometimes made for her. 'We always had the idea that children did it together. There was never anyone singled out,' says Dawn Lavender. 'But Hayley's class teacher came to me and said, "I think we should let Hayley sing a solo. I've never heard a child so tone true. She's perfect." It didn't mean anything to me, but I said, "You're the music person – fine." So we did.'

Jill remembers, 'I turned up with Gerald and Martine at the school hall and we got given the programme, which said *The Littlest Star* on the outside. And I opened it up and it said, "The Littlest Star: Hayley Westenra". And she hadn't said a thing. And suddenly, there she was up there – very composed, just like she is today. She walked calmly up to where she was supposed to stand and sang her song. You can imagine – my eyes watered.'

Martine Carter had her video camera and captured Hayley's first solo performance on tape. The video confirms that the voice was perfectly true. 'There is this little wee thing with such an accurate voice,' says Carter. 'It's not hugely strong, but she just has perfect pitch.'

Around this time another feature of Hayley's performing life was also established – the ability to carry on with preternatural

sang-froid when things went wrong. Martine Carter remembers: 'When she and Emma were about six or seven they were
in a ballet concert. There were four kids in the group. They had
to do one dance, and at the end were supposed to run to the
back of the stage to start the next one. But only three ran to the
back and Hayley was left at the front, standing there smiling at
the audience. She suddenly realised she was by herself. But she
didn't collapse, she just carried on.'

Fendalton Primary School also fostered musical ability in
talent quests, with heats during lunch hours and a final at the
annual school fair. Teachers knew that with the sort of support
Jill provided Hayley's act would always be well organised.

Talent quests would become a major training ground for her.
Some years later in London, Hayley's singing teacher asked her
how she got started. When Hayley mentioned talent quests, the
teacher said, 'Oh, you're one of those, are you?'

The quests helped develop a quietly determined competitiveness that would become a central feature of her character.
There was the odd occasion when Hayley would want to perform and a teacher would insist on letting someone else have a
turn, but in general staff did a good job of balancing the needs
of their star performer with the desire to give everyone an
opportunity.

'At times it's been hard for the teachers to treat her like
everyone else,' says a friend. 'Some worry they have to treat
her equally and go in the opposite direction, but other teachers
are fine about it.'

When it came time for Hayley to learn an instrument, her
class teacher had said that with her perfect pitch she should

take up the violin, so violin lessons had been arranged. A year later, the family bought a piano from a piano tuner and organised lessons with Janie Seed, the mother of one of Hayley's friends. Jill looked for teachers close to home to keep things simple: with violin, piano, the recorder and ballet to fit into the timetable, the simpler the better.

Janie taught Hayley, who is a more than competent pianist, for some eight years. She remembers her as 'obviously intelligent and musical, and very keen on her playing. It was no trouble getting her to practise, although even then she was very busy.' Hayley went through the grades of the Royal School of Music, then branched out into 'the kind of music she likes singing. She'd look for things where she could accompany herself.'

Jill and Gerald chose nearby Cobham Intermediate when it was time for Hayley to move on from primary school. She sailed through lessons with her now customary aplomb, and music still took up a large part of her time. Like Fendalton Primary, Cobham placed a lot of emphasis on music. The late John Haberfield was the teacher in charge of music. 'He came to me and said, "I've heard the most fabulous voice with absolutely perfect pitch,"' says Hayley's teacher Lois Butler.

Hayley was placed in a class for students of high ability. The school had an orchestra, a choir, a chorale, a chamber group drawn from the orchestra, a jazz group and a dance group – Hayley was part of all of them. And she didn't use these commitments as an excuse to get out of other activities, to which she also gave 100 per cent.

'She was a tiny girl,' says Butler, 'but she was very fit. I remember her once doing a cross-country run on a school camp. The biggest boy in the class was prone and she was leaning over him, encouraging him to get up and carry on. She has unbounded energy.' Which she needed. 'She was so involved with so much that she wasn't the best at getting things done on time.' It's about the most severe criticism of Hayley you will hear from a teacher. 'I can understand why, because she was a perfectionist. There was no, "Oh I'll just get this done." She always kept away at anything till she got it right.'

About this time, Hayley decided to give up karate lessons.

Like Fendalton Primary, Cobham Intermediate had an annual musical production. As soon as she saw Hayley, the school's drama teacher decided to build a show around her. *Alice in Wonderland* was the result, and a great success. Most people who were lucky enough to attend one of the performances made three observations: Hayley could really sing, she could really act and she looked like she was going to go a long way.

A lot of children who are fortunate enough to have a gift like Hayley's have little time for those who aren't so lucky. Hayley has never been one of those children. Janie Seed remembers taking her own daughter, Julia, and other schoolmates in her car with Hayley. 'They were talking about their parts in *Alice in Wonderland*, and it came up that my daughter was doing the scenery painting. And Hayley said, "Julia, that's so wonderful that you're painting the scenery. You're so good at art." She was always so supportive of her friends.'

Hayley's friends from this time are still her friends today. They were naturally drawn to the girl with the generous personality and infectious giggle she has never lost. 'She always had a smile on her face, even when things were tough,' says principal Trevor Beaton. He describes her as 'a sheer delight, even before the singing talent was apparent to us. She related well to everyone, she was thoroughly motivated, and though she wasn't an athlete, she gave everything a go. We said she would be famous one day, but also that she would never change. And she hasn't. Celebrity hasn't made her superior in any way.'

After two years at Cobham, it was time for Hayley and her friends to move on to high school. 'At final assembly – I don't think anyone who attended will ever forget – she sang "Time to Say Goodbye",' says Beaton. 'And there was not a dry eye in the place. It must have been hard for her to do, but she carried it off.'

Around this time, in a casebook example of the advisability of being careful what one wishes for, Jill began to feel life was getting a little dull.

'I said to Gerald, "Let's do something exciting." We were saving up for a Tiki Tour. We hadn't done anything adventuresome. We'd always played it safe. I thought, why not uproot and do something while the children are young? I looked at these photos of Ireland and it reminded me of my own childhood, so I got inspired by Ireland. There were photos of people busking in the streets. I thought that would be a good environment for the children. I did look into getting an Irish passport, but we didn't even have the money to go there to check it out.'

Jill felt that ten years of child-rearing had passed by in a very predictable way, and she didn't want the next ten years to be the same. They would not be.

CHAPTER TWO

Busk Stop

Hayley was still at intermediate school when she began busking. The very first occasion was when she was taking part in a concert at the Christchurch Arts Centre. Lunchtime arrived and no one had any money, so Hayley sang for her supper. It was such a success that it became a regular part of the weekend's activities for Hayley and Sophie, who has a fine voice of her own.

Christchurch is New Zealand's busking capital, with an annual busking festival that draws performers (and now tourists) from all over the world, though not Hayley Westenra – it favours more eccentric acts than hers. But even in an environment where busking is accepted as part of the city's fabric, street performance is tough work. It's you and the audience – or sometimes no audience – with no introduction, no guarantee that anyone will stop and listen, and no guarantee of financial gain. Hayley did very well at it.

Busking taught her some vital lessons for a performer, including choosing the right material for the audience and pacing the selections to hold a crowd's interest. One thing she didn't need to learn was confidence: right from the start the spotlight was where she belonged.

Now 167cm tall, Hayley's growth spurt came late, and in the early days passersby would be stopped in their tracks by the strength of the voice emanating from the tiny girl who seemed to have nowhere on her form from which to produce it. Occasionally more seasoned performers would give Hayley the benefit of their experience. At one busking competition, clowns Carrot and Pickle watched, impressed. Whether it was Carrot or Pickle who spoke, no one can quite remember, but one of them told her that he had noticed that the crowd would thin out during the violin solos Hayley used in her act. She took his advice to reduce the numbers she played on the violin in favour of singing.

Jill helped her choose material and observed how the crowd reacted. She was sensitive to the possibility people might think the girl's parents were sending her out to earn money for them, especially if one of them was hovering nearby, but she thought it important that she be there to support and protect her.

Hayley's legend has it that she was 'discovered' busking and scooped up to be made an international star. It's so much a part of the mythology that it's a rare film crew profiling Hayley – whether in New Zealand, New York or London – that doesn't ask her to sing on the street for their item. The reality of her 'discovery' is more complicated, but it is true that without paying her dues on the streets of Christchurch she would not be the performer she is today.

Christchurch is a city of strong musical traditions dating back to the nineteenth century, when a fierce rivalry developed between the choirs of its two cathedrals. It has produced many of New Zealand's finest singers – Richard Greager, Christopher Doig and Malcolm McNeill among them. Today that legacy can be seen in schools that foster musical talent, in busking festivals and in a culture of talent quests which does not exist elsewhere in New Zealand. Several of the city's shopping malls hold competitions for young performers in the school holidays, and these are taken seriously indeed, and supported by an infrastructure of drama, dance and music schools, as well as by parents like Jill Westenra and young performers like Hayley.

As with everything else to which she turned her hand, once Hayley decided to compete in talent quests, she would compete to the best of her ability. And competition was intense. Jill helped with all the support she could. She spent hours in the library looking for suitable songs, and always took home the maximum number of books allowed. She was savvy enough to seek out songs to which people had an emotional attachment, as well as numbers that would showcase the special qualities of Hayley's voice. And she worked well in advance, giving Hayley plenty of time to decide what to wear and find musical arrangements. Nonetheless, mother and daughter didn't always see eye to eye on Jill's selections. 'Oh Mum, that's so old. It's your era,' Hayley would say, dismissing one of Jill's cherished choices.

Not all the children competing in the quests had their parents in the audience. But Hayley did. And friends like Martine Carter were brought along as well. She was there the day Hayley learned a lesson which looms large in the family account of her career.

'It was a talent quest in South City,' recalls Carter. 'She opened her mouth and it was wrong. Jill and I just looked at each other, because Hayley never sings out of tune. She kept going for the first verse, then you could see her thinking, This isn't right. She put it in the right key as she went into the next verse.'

'The intro was just one note,' explains Jill. 'And the crowd was so noisy she couldn't hear it. Looking back she should have stopped it and explained, but she was so young she didn't know that. She didn't get through to the semi-finals and was very upset that people would think she couldn't sing. She moped on the way home in the car and burst into tears in her room. I said, "Let's learn from this."'

Part of Jill wanted not to tempt fate by taking Hayley's talent for granted. 'Even when she won and did well,' says Carter, 'Jill kept saying to me, "Do you think she's really good? Am I just biased?" Lots of people have good voices and look gorgeous, like Hayley. But she's got that other thing that makes her stand out.'

Jill grew weary of seeing Hayley perform her best but come runner-up to a tap dancer or a boy doing the moon walk. But if the tap dancer won, it only made Hayley more determined to do better. Part of the problem may have been that she made her performance seem so effortless that the judges weren't aware of how much work had gone into it. But as she got more experience under her belt, Hayley learned more about what would please an audience. And the family worked to finesse the details that would make the difference between doing well and doing best.

After each competition there would be a post-mortem back at the Westenra house. It was a shared hobby. The family tried to think of what Hayley could do to improve her chances, perhaps adding a dance, or working on the acting side of things.

Hayley had been competing in the quests for two years before she finally scored a first place, at the Northlands Mall Talent Quest in 1998, singing 'Mists of Islay'. She won $1750, a useful, not to say encouraging sum for an eleven-year-old, as well as $1000 for her school.

Jill proved ingenious at devising ways around the core problem of juvenile repertoire: the fact that most popular songs are about adult romantic love. She would look for a child's equivalent of the feeling being expressed in the song. So when, for instance, Hayley sang Lloyd Webber's 'Wishing You Were Somehow Here Again' in a talent quest, Jill told her to imagine she was singing it about an absent father.

Little mistakes were major disappointments. Hayley was devastated when on one occasion the family turned up to a quest to find she was a week late and the heats had already been held. She was told she could perform but not compete. Hayley wasn't interested in that. She says she took the competitions seriously right from the start.

'When you do something you want to do your best,' she explains. 'I found it really annoying that I'd always come second. When I finally came first it was great.'

Although it looks as though every opportunity to perform was taken, Jill can still remember the talent quests in which Hayley didn't compete because they didn't know about them – and what the prizes were. They were doubly disappointed when, after a skiing holiday, they turned up too late to one that Hayley had competed in the previous year only to be told, 'What a shame – she would have won this year.'

Hayley won prizes like an hour's free singing, drama and dancing lessons, or CD vouchers, the last of which led to a fateful purchase. 'I got these CD vouchers for winning this talent quest,' says Hayley. 'The first album I picked up was by Andrea Bocelli and I really enjoyed it. Then I started singing his songs an octave higher. Those were the kind of songs that really worked. He's kind of crossover. Right from when I was young I was into crossover between classical and pop. By just searching for the right song you discover other styles, and it was really beneficial when it came to the point of recording a whole album and knowing what songs worked for me and what didn't.'

As well as the school music, busking and talent quests there were still more outlets for Hayley's talent. She briefly did singing telegrams, which brought her a tidy amount of pocket money, and she appeared in many local musical productions. She had seen some children performing in *Cinderella* and asked, 'How do you get to do that? I want to do that.'

'She didn't want to go into learning anything,' says Jill. 'She wanted to do it. She wanted to dress up in costume and get on stage.'

The first, in 1995, was *Annie*, which with its small army of parts for orphan girls has been the starting point for many aspiring musical theatre performers. Hayley auditioned and won the part of Kate (The Orphan Who Holds up the Mouse). Sophie, aged just four, won a part too, as the smallest of the orphans.

Jill did not have the show business background that meant she knew just what to do to get her daughter into shows. Like Hayley, she has had to learn as she has gone along. It was Martine Carter who noticed that auditions were advertised in the newspaper, and in 1996 saw one for *The Sound of Music*. Hayley auditioned and was immediately cast as Marta. She seemed to know instinctively how to act – to stand back and not grab all the attention.

Occasionally, it was Sophie who set out to get a part and Hayley who ended up in a production as an afterthought. Such was the case with *Rush*, a successful musical about Otago gold-fever days. Hayley went along to support her sister at the audition and thought it looked like so much fun that she got a part, as did Sophie and Isaac.

They must have been quite good at auditions. Though Hayley says she was never confident of winning a part, she learned much later that others' hearts sank when the Westenras turned up to apply for a role.

But, though *Annie* and *The Sound of Music* were enjoyable, singing show tunes was not where Hayley's heart lay. 'When I was younger,' she says today, 'it was one of the outlets for my singing and the acting and dancing. I enjoyed being with other children and dressing up and going on stage. It was lots of fun.

But I'm enjoying the music I'm singing now more compared to show music.'

Opera was another possibility. Hayley appeared several times with Canterbury Opera, whose productions normally feature a children's chorus. Competition for places is hard fought. But that involvement was short-lived as the developing singer found herself, after early solo roles such as an urchin in *La Bohème* and Tiny Tim in *A Christmas Carol*, increasingly consigned to group work. The children's roles were also kept simple, and for a musician of Hayley's developing abilities there was no challenge. The parts – many of them boys' roles – that were made available for her started to appeal less and less, and her involvement tapered off.

Nonetheless, ten-year-old Hayley was busy in 1997. Among other performances she appeared in *The Witches*, *The Darling Buds of May*, *The King and I* (as a Siamese twin), *A Christmas Carol* and *The Nutcracker*. The last was with the New Zealand Ballet, but Hayley was disappointed to find she was a boy again and wouldn't get to wear a pretty dress. Another of her more memorable stage appearances that year was in an Australian production of *Snow White and the Seven Dwarfs*, which found itself in Christchurch a couple of dwarves short. Somehow the show had managed to muster only five little people instead of the requisite seven. Hayley's ballet teacher, Patricia Paul, had provided local dancers for the touring show. Could she rustle up a brace of dwarves? She immediately thought of Hayley and Sophie, and contacted Jill, who got her daughters out of school to present themselves for consideration.

Although Hayley was almost too tall to be a dwarf, the sisters were accepted and found themselves slinging their picks on their shoulders (in Hayley's case, Jill remembers, the wrong shoulder) and singing 'Hi Ho, Hi Ho' with their older but not taller counterparts. Not long after their début, a genuine dwarf was located, but Hayley and Sophie were allowed to continue in the production, alternating their part.

Both the children had performed in well-run, professionally managed productions, but this was something different. There was only one rehearsal and there appeared to be a dispute about payment, which didn't involve them, going on behind the scenes. The main lesson Hayley took from the experience was that what might appear to the audience to be a smooth-run show could be anything but backstage. The professional's job was to rise above the difference.

Not that Hayley was precious about what she would or wouldn't do. She would try anything if it meant she got to per-form. During 1996 she tried her hand at modelling, which developed both discipline and confidence. She did catalogue work and TV commercials. And she learned that modelling was hard work. One ad in which she appeared was made in Christchurch's chilly winter but shot to appear like summer. She had to bounce around in an icy swimming pool and was starting to turn blue before she was allowed to get into a shower to warm up.

While Hayley was already notching up remarkable successes for her age, not everything went her way. At the end of 1996 the possibility of a part in an Australian film, *Amy*, became a family preoccupation to the extent that it ruined a summer holiday.

Even before leaving home, the project had proved complicated.

Hayley had to supply a video audition tape, which saw Jill rigging up lights in the living room and shooting with a borrowed camera till two in the morning. It was only afterwards that she remembered that one of the family's neighbours was a TVNZ cameraman.

Although Jill remembers the tape as an amateurish affair, it was good enough to get Hayley on a short list of three girls for a substantial part in the movie. One was in Auckland, one in London and one – Hayley – in a tent. The Westenras were on a camping holiday at the time the decision was to be made, and the suspense cast a shadow over their vacation as they checked daily with the camping-ground office to see if there was any news. First the Auckland girl was dropped, then the London hopeful was out and the Auckland one back in. Eventually the part went to a young Sydney actress.

The self-doubt that is part of Hayley's story came into play as everyone wondered why she hadn't been good enough to get the part. When the Westenras finally got to see the movie they realised Hayley hadn't been small enough.

The Westenras had to give up camping holidays when Hayley started to become well known. Children would recognise her and follow her around the camping ground, forcing her to retreat under canvas with a book if she was to get any peace. And on one occasion, a man stared at Jill through a bathroom window while she was brushing her teeth because he 'had to see what Hayley Westenra's mum looked like'.

It was a talent quest on a grand scale that had brought Hayley to the notice of an audience outside Christchurch. The

McDonald's Young Entertainers television contest was a popular showcase for junior talent that ran for several years in the late 1990s. Hayley did well when she competed, but once again the diversity of talent on offer meant that she was an apple being judged against oranges.

Nevertheless, in 1999 she reached the finals, which were filmed on the marae at Te Papa in Wellington. Hayley's performance earned her 48 out of a possible 50 points. This seemed to bode well, but she didn't realise that such contests are always marked high. Hers turned out to be the lowest score, and she finished fourth. An all-male vocal group won.

Jill agrees that occasional losses were good for developing Hayley's character and taught her how to accept disappointment. And in this case the disappointment was mitigated when *TV Guide* magazine published a slew of letters from viewers saying Hayley should have won.

While taking part in McDonald's Young Entertainers, Hayley encountered local McDonald's franchisee Alan Traill, a music lover and arts patron. When Hayley reached the semi-finals of the national competition it was brought to Traill's attention that there was a Christchurch performer involved. 'It was suggested I might like to touch base and offer assistance,' says Traill. 'I did exactly that and made every effort I could to be helpful at that stage. I remember a day at The Palms shopping centre when she competed. She was such a tiny thing – there was nothing of her. But even at that age, she sang and danced with such confidence in front of a huge crowd and TV cameras and judges.'

That admiration soon extended to admiration for the Westenra family's attitudes and philosophies. 'It wasn't long before both my wife Netti and I warmed to the family. It grew very quickly well beyond the business side.'

The more he knew of Hayley, the more impressed Traill became. 'When the [McDonald's Young Entertainers] troupe were in Christchurch, they used to come round to our home. Hayley sang one night when a professional group was there. She was certainly the equal of them.'

Other supporters from the early years have stayed loyal to Hayley and she to them. Hers is a personality that makes people want to help. The first time Hayley needed a gown for a performance, the search began for an expert to point them in the right direction. Fashion designer Sonya Smith was based not far from Gerald's shop, so he called in one day to ask if she knew of anyone who would be interested in making a one-off gown. Smith had not heard of the young singer but was intrigued by the project, and Hayley put herself in Smith's design hands.

'I didn't know many people in Christchurch who could do this, so I just went with it,' says Smith. 'Hayley was only fourteen, so I had to make her look gorgeous and glamorous without making her look tacky. She had to look homegrown, natural and innocent. But she had a beautiful body, and was very easy for a designer to dress.'

Hayley made a point of thanking Sonya publicly whenever the opportunity arose for a long time afterwards. 'She designs a new outfit for every performance and they're all gorgeous!!! A very big THANK YOU to Sonya who I couldn't do without!!!!' she told one interviewer.

For her part, Smith describes all her work as 'a labour of love', a description justified not just because she never charged

Hayley for any of the dresses but also because of the work she put into them. Her description of one gown is typical: 'a stand-out was a beautiful soft lilac dupion silk, boned bodice and very full skirt with netting underneath. Then I hand-dyed and hand-made little butterflies to put all over the skirt and they were dyed in the same lilac. Then I hand-dyed, again in lilac to match, soft tulle netting with a huge voluminous wrap, and it just looked so ethereal and beautiful.

'Seeing [the design] do what it's meant to do fills me with pride,' says Smith. 'When I see her on stage I'm not looking or listening immediately to her voice. I'm checking everything is sitting perfect. Once I'm happy in my head then I can hear the voice.' And like everyone else, Smith describes Hayley as 'a joy to work with. I've never seen her frown.'

As the partnership developed, the demands on Hayley's time required new ways of working. 'In the end it was easier for me to work around her for fittings than for her to change her schedule. We would do fittings at home. She would answer the door and squeal when she saw it, and run her girly run to the bedroom and try it on before her mother saw it.'

As with the choice of musical material, Hayley's age put limits on clothing material. Black, with its connotations of adult sexiness was out, though Smith had a timeline planned for introducing a progressively more adult look. Her one regret is that Hayley's overseas commitments have meant they can no longer work together as they used to.

Someone else who helped Hayley with her look for these early appearances was hairdresser Mike Hamel, who was aware of Hayley from an appearance on *60 Minutes*. 'I thought, there's a young girl who needs some looking after so she can grow and be a world-class entertainer.' He contacted her and offered to look after her hair at no charge. Hayley was delighted and bemused at the something-for-nothing offer, but Hamel explained he respected success and loved to support talent. He also has a hairdresser's natural enthusiasm for Hayley's locks. 'She's got beautiful long hair,' he says, 'which I've often curled or straightened with a flat iron, or sometimes left very natural. She's the perfect specimen for the girl next door. It suits her personality – she's not trying to be someone she's not. She is natural.'

In return for his support, Hayley has credited Ginger Meggs Hair Design in her promotional material, and even after she had signed an international record deal with Decca UK she made a point of performing in the salon one Christmas to show her gratitude.

CHAPTER THREE

The Memento

Paradoxically, Hayley's first recording was made not because her family expected her to go on to have a major career, but in case she did not. The germ of the idea was planted by a man who had become a fan of Hayley's from her McDonald's Young Entertainers performances. He began to send postcards – which he does to this day – and in one suggested that it would be wonderful to have a recording of Hayley's young voice as a memento. The family thought this an excellent idea.

Naturally, neither Jill nor Hayley knew anything about recording. Equally naturally, Jill set herself the task of learning whatever she needed to know to make it happen. A recording engineer the family knew told them he had spare time in his studio. It was the school holidays, so a good time for Hayley too.

'We'd been thinking about it,' says Jill, 'and said, "Let's just do it." If we'd thought about the cost and the work involved, we might not have done anything.'

The tracks chosen for the album, made in 2000, were staples of Hayley's busking act and talent quest performances, a heterodox mix of show tunes, pop and hits by Hayley's beloved Andrea Bocelli. The full track listing is: 'Con te Partiro', 'La Luna Che Non C'e', 'Il Mare Calmo Della Sera', 'Another Suitcase in Another Hall', 'Unexpected Song', 'Memory', 'Wishing You Were Somehow Here Again', 'The Mists of Islay', 'Walking in the Air', 'Pie Jesu', 'How Deep Is Your Love', 'Groovy Kind of Love' and 'Eternal Flame'.

Once the selection was made, backings had to be found. There was no question of being able to afford to pay musicians, but technology came to the rescue. Midi files were sourced off the Internet, and a technology-minded acquaintance, Arnie Van Bussel, modified them to suit Hayley.

The Westenras paid for some seventy copies of *Walking in the Air* to give to family members and special friends. But of course, once you have a compact disc you need a cover. Having taught herself to be a record producer, Jill now had to become a graphic designer. She became consumed by the CD. She had started a watercolour painting course, but she had to give it up because she couldn't concentrate. Instead, her mind was dwelling on the artwork for the album. That she wasn't an expert only made her feel more pressure. So she took up studying photography, which remains a passion – and a possible future career – to this day. Some of Jill's photography is now being used for official Hayley purposes, including the cover of this book.

Jill found the perfect location for the cover shot: a beach at sunrise with a misty, mystical air that would convey perfectly the ethereality of Hayley's young voice. One morning she was there, planning where she would take the shots, and met a woman walking her dog. 'This is just amazing,' said Jill. 'It is amazing,' said the woman. 'I've lived here three years and I've never seen it like this before.' Jill decided to take her chances anyway, and that weekend the family plus home-made reflectors and all the other necessary gear headed off to the beach before dawn. 'And there was no mist,' says Jill. 'But we had breakfast and watched the sunrise with the kids, which was amazing for them.'

Which just goes to show that there is no such thing as a wasted experience for her family where Jill Westenra is concerned. Eventually, the cover photo was taken at a farmlet belonging to an aunt.

The last stage in the process was the choice of a name. Again, Jill professes, she had no idea what the criteria were for choosing an album title. The recording engineer, Rob Mayes, pointed out that many CDs were titled after the name of one of their tracks, and *Walking in the Air* seemed to sum up perfectly both the quality of Hayley's voice and the music on the disc. But though hers is an exceptional voice, the Hayley who sings on *Walking in the Air* is an extraordinarily gifted twelve-year-old, not a fully developed singer.

In due course the CD was completed, a remarkably professional product considering it was the work of a group of people who had no idea what they were going to have to do when they embarked on the project.

One of the people to whom they wanted to give a copy was Alan Traill. 'The family came around proudly to give me a copy of the CD,' he recalls, 'which I didn't even know they were doing. My copy is numbered No. 1. I played it, and because I am so respectful and recognising of Hayley's talent I love that CD.'

Hayley was still busking frequently at this time and her audience would often ask if she had a CD they could buy. The idea of producing a greater number of copies to sell began to take shape. Alan Traill learned that the family had considered making more copies but the cost was prohibitive and the idea had been shelved. Anyway, the CD had served its purpose of providing them with a memento of Hayley as she sounded at age twelve.

'But Netti and I could see the potential,' says Traill. 'And I guess in those early days we used to spend a lot of time with them talking about what might happen with Hayley. So we said, "Why don't you let us fund this and see what happens?" And they were hesitant at first, but at the end of the day they agreed and I funded the production of that first 1000 copies of *Walking in the Air*.'

Walking in the Air, like the talent quests and the musicals and the busking, had become an enjoyable family project. 'When you look back, it was exciting times,' says Jill of that period. 'It was fun.'

As one friend has observed: 'What's happened with Hayley just seems a natural progression. The family is always very focused on what they do and the kids always come first, no matter what. Gerald and Jill wouldn't be the sort of people

Hayley as a baby with her parents Jill and Gerald Westenra, 1988.

Hayley helps Granddad Ireland play the piano accordian, 1989. Gerry Ireland could play almost any instrument by ear and his wife, Shirley, had a fine voice, which family members describe as remarkably similar to Hayley's.

Proud Shirley Ireland and granddaughter Hayley in Timaru, 1988.

Hayley, age two, on the slide at Tahunanui playground, Nelson,
with 'Baby Rose', her constant companion.

Trying out her new radio and microphone.

Her first lead solo singing performance, at six years of age in Fendalton Primary School's Christmas production of *The Littlest Star*, 1993.
This was where Hayley's extraordinary talent was first recognised.

Hayley (seven) with her brother Isaac (one) and sister Sophie (four) enjoying one of their many tea parties, 1994.

A Christmas ballet performance with Hayley second from left, 1994. Dancing and musical theatre were passions that she also pursued at a young age.

Performing at the Caroline Bay Carnival, Timaru, 1999. By age eleven,
Hayley had performed in more than 40 stage productions.

Busking at the Arts Centre in Christchurch, 2001, with Isaac and Sophie.

Singing teacher and mentor Dame Malvina Major came to hear Hayley in concert in 2001 and called backstage. They share a close and treasured relationship.

who'd be into socialising on the weekend and going off and leaving their kids. They enjoy their kids.'

One copy of *Walking in the Air* went to the man whose idea the CD was. Others were sold on the street while busking. And nothing was too much trouble: Jill had sold the last of one batch of CDs when a young couple came by and wanted to buy a copy. Seeing their disappointment when they learned that day's supply was sold out, she delivered a copy to their hotel that night. (That Hayley Westenra is still the same thoughtful and unpretentious person today that she was then is shown by the fact that long after the success of her album *Pure* she was concerned that she would not be able to accept an invitation from that same couple to sing at their wedding.)

But there was more work to come. With 1000 copies of a CD to offload, Jill had to learn about marketing. She noted that record stores had posters of artists they were selling, so posters were made for *Walking in the Air*, and Gerald found himself doing poster runs after work at night. Needless to say, original copies of *Walking in the Air* are now highly prized collectors' items.

'We didn't think the CD would lead to anything beyond what it was,' says Jill. But with nothing to lose, they sent copies out to radio stations and the media. Little interest was shown at first, though an obscure station, Christchurch Plains FM, was the first to play one of the tracks. That was an exciting day in the Westenra household.

One of the shops Jill was wont to frequent when looking for karaoke backings for her children's performances was The Record Room, owned by Rod Mitchell. He had known the family since he and his wife Fiona had attended antenatal classes with the Westenras when Jill was pregnant with Hayley. They had been friends ever since. He had watched Hayley develop through the busking and talent quests.

'Jill left me a copy of the CD,' says Mitchell, 'and wanted to know what I thought of it. So we played it in the shop, and it got an instant response. Everyone wanted to know who it was, so we offered to put it in the shop.'

Mitchell found a photo of Hayley and put it up with the legend 'Guess who?', which attracted more interest. He also marketed it through his store advertising over several months. 'We ended up selling more copies of that than the chart albums we had in stock some weeks.' As well as the quality of the music, buyers were intrigued by the youth of the performer. Many were also starting to draw the comparison with UK teen soprano Charlotte Church that would become so familiar to Hayley, her family and her record company – all of whom would deal with it in their own ways.

Another early enthusiast for *Walking in the Air* was Gerald's business partner, Polish émigré Jacek (Jack) Pawlowski, a conspicuously courteous and sophisticated European of the old school. Through his contacts in the local Polish community, he knew Australian-resident conductor Vladimir Kamirski, who occasionally conducted in Christchurch.

'Once he came to visit our shop,' relates Pawlowski. 'Gerald gave him the disc to listen to. He went quiet. His face changed. He went white. After a couple of songs he said, "Who teach her Italian? It's perfect."'

Kamirski did some pacing, went outside and smoked a

cigarette, and came back in. 'He said, "Gerald, you wasting your and her time. Close the shop. Sell the house or mortgage it and go to London. Do it and I want only 10 per cent."'

In the event, Hayley would get to London without the house being sold, although Gerald would give up his share of the shop in the process. Kamirski offered to advance Hayley's career in Sydney, but the performer was too young and the distance between the cities proved a difficulty. Gerald says he's glad now that Hayley did not attempt her first overseas steps at that age. 'In my opinion the wonderful thing is that this all didn't come to this level at a younger age. Then she'd be hallmarked with the child prodigy label, which is really hard to throw out. Charlotte Church wants to change her direction, but she's stuck with that label.'

Kamirski, however, did provide some enthusiastic encomia that were printed for stickers attached to the *Walking in the Air* cover, as well as to Hayley's next CD – a marketing ploy Alan Traill had suggested.

Meanwhile, Alan Traill's financial support had not been forgotten. 'I offered to pay full stop,' explains Traill. 'They [the Westenras] had gone away feeling a bit uncomfortable, and I was worried they might say no and that would stymie the potential. So I went back a day or two later with a Plan B, which was to underwrite it. That was the arrangement we had. Then a year or so later, they came back with a cheque. And at that point I said, "Look, this was never intended to be underwriting. It was a gift to assist Hayley," and I gave it back to them. I said, "Use the money now for the next step." Their reaction to the initial offer of the gift says a lot – some folk would have snapped it up. Looking back, I'm proud of myself for coming up with Plan B.'

So at thirteen Hayley was a talented youngster with a CD to her name and a small but enthusiastic regional following. Soon she would be a talented fourteen-year-old with a record deal.

CHAPTER FOUR

Hayley Westenra

'People told us we should send *Walking in the Air* to Paul Holmes,' says Gerald. 'Hayley sent one with a letter to him, but it went missing or something. We couriered copies off to Mushroom Australia, Sony NZ and Australia, EMI, Warners, Universal. Jill would ring on a weekly basis. "Have you heard it yet?" "No, we'll get round to it."'

Then Gray Bartlett MBE, a performer, producer and now promoter of many decades' experience, took an interest. A publicist friend had heard Hayley singing on a local TV station and rung him. 'She said, "Gray, I've seen someone you should take notice of. She's fantastic,"' recalls Bartlett. 'I said, "Get her to send some stuff to me."' The friend did so, and Bartlett recognised Hayley's quality immediately. He describes it now as the sort of talent that comes along once in a decade.

With his history and connections Bartlett was able to break through the walls Jill had been bashing her head against. Universal's staff had listened to *Walking in the Air* and liked it but hadn't got back to the Westenras. Bartlett knew Universal's boss, George Ash, and called to encourage him to take Hayley on.

But he had already pulled another string. Instead of going first to the record company, he contacted his friend Mike Valintine, a *60 Minutes* journalist, and persuaded him to listen to *Walking in the Air*. Valintine was impressed and agreed to do a story on Hayley.

The commercial value of fifteen minutes of positive coverage on a programme with the cachet of *60 Minutes* is difficult to calculate. Bartlett, with a promoter's enthusiasm, estimates it at $350,000, which is probably a little on the high side, but an accurate figure would still be in the tens of thousands. Whatever the amount, his move meant that when he did finally sit down with George Ash he had not only an artist and a recording but also a swag of free publicity with which to launch her.

'I thought, I just want to go to one record company where I've got a friend,' says Bartlett. 'One was Warners, the other was George Ash at Universal. So I went to George.'

Here, things get a little murky. Who appreciated what aspect of Hayley's talent at what point, and who had the legal right to develop that talent's commercial potential, has been a matter of some dispute. It's perhaps best, and most accurate, to say that an accord was reached – an accord which resulted in Hayley Westenra becoming a Universal recording artist.

Before anything could happen, however, Hayley and Universal had to meet and see if they liked each other. She and Jill were flown up to Auckland where they were met by company A&R man Grant Kearney.

Mother and daughter were independently having the same thoughts as Kearney drove them to town: that he would be more used to driving exciting rock stars around and that he – and the record company – might find them a little bit . . . square.

Then Kearney surprised them both in a way many other music industry figures would over the years. He showed that his first interest was in Hayley's welfare by expressing concern for her education. Performing commitments were inevitably eating into class time. He also revealed an appreciation for her voice.

Hayley's worries that her quiet personality and demure looks wouldn't make the necessary impact were needless. They liked her for who she was. They also liked her because of her voice. Everyone at Universal who heard it was impressed by the purity, accuracy and sheer musicality of Hayley's singing. That she was only thirteen years old was a minor factor by comparison with the maturity of her musicianship.

Plan A was to use *Walking in the Air* as the basis for a Universal release, giving the vocals a bit of a polish and using the same backings. It would not have been unattractive to a record company to have a new artist arrive with the financial advantage of a completed product. But on closer examination this proved to be impossible. There were technical and legal difficulties with using the existing backings, and a new recording would have to be made.

Several of the tracks from *Walking in the Air* were re-recorded by producer David Selfe and engineer Greg O'Donnell for the album that would be released under the name *Hayley Westenra*: 'Walking in the Air', 'Memory', 'The Mists of Islay', 'Wishing You Were Somehow Here Again' and, of course, 'Pie Jesu'. To these were added both Bach's and Schubert's 'Ave Maria', 'All I Ask of You', 'Somewhere', 'Bright Eyes', 'I Dreamed a Dream' and 'Love Changes Everything'. There were also bonus tracks of 'Amazing Grace' and 'God Defend New Zealand', which Hayley also sang in Maori – a practice that has become a staple of her performances wherever she goes.

It was exciting for Hayley to feel she was in the hands of experts. And with that came the trimmings. She had her first professional photo shoot, which she anticipated with the same nerves she had felt when meeting her first glamorous record company executive. Weren't photographers used to photographing models, not Christchurch schoolgirls? But the photographer's first words – that she was good 'raw material'– both disarmed her and put her at ease.

Hayley let herself be guided by the more experienced music industry personnel when it came to the track selection. She assumed the record company would know more about making records than she did. The Westenra family's choices on *Walking in the Air* formed the blueprint, but the relatively obscure Italian selections were the first to go.

'David Selfe and I took ages making sure it had the right combination of tracks,' says Gray Bartlett, who is credited as executive producer. He had noted that Canadian producer David Foster, who had made landmark recordings with the likes of Barbra Streisand and Josh Groban, always included a track coupling the singer with another name artist. Bartlett had an association with the Royal Scots Dragoons, whose version of 'Amazing Grace' breathed new life into that chestnut when it became a worldwide hit for them in 1972. So Hayley was taken to Hamilton and recorded 'Amazing Grace' live with a bevy of bagpipers.

Bartlett and Selfe added touches here and there, but Bartlett says, 'I think it's important that what's happened with Hayley is a combination of her immense talent, her determination to pull it off and her commitment to her art form.'

Hayley was delighted with the result but had the odd quibble. She felt, for instance, that the version of 'Pie Jesu' was faster than it should be. But she was a young teenager and working with industry veterans. Her input was minor. There would be plenty of opportunities to do that particular number the way she thought best in the next few years.

It's music industry orthodoxy that the best title for a début album is the artist's name, reinforcing the performer's identity in the public's mind. *Hayley Westenra* was recorded quickly, completed in time for a Mother's Day release, targeting one of Hayley's largest potential audiences: kids and their mums.

The *60 Minutes* piece on Hayley aired in the week after the album's release. And the next day, says Universal's marketing manager Alister Cain, 'people were queuing up at The Warehouse to buy the album'. Within two months it had sold 45,000 copies. In New Zealand, a sale of 15,000 copies – the size of the album's first pressing – qualifies for platinum status.

Used to dealing with gangsta wannabes and putative punk-poppers, Universal's marketing skills were stretched by Hayley. They knew the audience was out there; the problem was connecting them with their artist. She came under the aegis of Cain whose responsibility was 'strategic, classics and jazz' – which meant that, in his words, it was nice to have a live one to work with.

'I had a really open mind about categorising her,' he says, 'because I think if you just target her in an older demographic you're really limiting her. We know she has fans her own age. So we put spots on TV2, which is a big call, and some on TV3 because her appeal is so broad. Not every teenage girl or boy likes Korn. There's others like Hayley out there.'

The classical music market has changed enormously in the past few years. The dabbling of artists like Kiri Te Kanawa and Luciano Pavarotti in show tunes and easy-listening numbers paved the way for the genre-defying style that came to be called 'crossover', appealing to sections of both the classical and pop markets. This is where Hayley's talents lay, and although at this stage no one had quite realised it, her timing was perfect. To put it brutally, crossover would save the classical recording industry.

Cain also recognised that many people have wider tastes than record companies traditionally give them credit for. 'Pigeonholing her would have been dangerous, and I just felt we should market it to everyone. Hayley can go and do an amazing recital,' says Cain, 'but she can also sing "Wuthering Heights".'

Everyone expected the album to do well, but no one guessed just how well. The biggest problem with *Hayley Westenra* was ensuring shops had enough copies to keep up with the demand. Fortunately, the discs were pressed locally and stocks could be topped up quickly.

On the back of the album's success, a national tour was arranged, packaged by Bartlett and his partner Ian Magan. Hayley sang in seven centres, supported by tenor Shaun Dixon, baritone Tim Beveridge and, at Hayley's suggestion, her friend, fourteen-year-old violin prodigy Ben Morrison. Local school choirs provided support in each venue. And, in another pattern that would be repeated over the years, Sophie and Isaac also joined her on stage.

The tour allowed the rest of New Zealand to see what Christchurch audiences already knew. Gray Bartlett identified a key to Hayley's appeal. 'She's an idyllic role model. Wouldn't you love her to be your daughter? And kids love her because they think, "Oh my God, this could happen to me." That's a large part of the market, and no one's doing anything for them.'

Young girls in particular look up to Hayley for inspiration. And so do boys. Hayley doesn't find being a role model a strain because it's simply a matter of being who she is. 'I've had quite a few letters from people who say they've been inspired by me,' she says. 'It's a nice feeling. Coming from Christchurch is another thing – it's not like another person from Auckland or overseas. It's like, if she's been able to do it, well maybe I can too.'

For her part, Hayley cites numerous influences, starting close to home. 'Both my parents have been role models, but Mum more,' she says. 'If she hadn't encouraged me, I wouldn't have thought, I can do this. I think I always thought, Well, I'll try really hard but I probably won't get there, and Mum's the one who said, "You can do this, Hayley, and you've got the ability. Why not go ahead and do it?"'

Musically, Andrea Bocelli is top of her list of inspirations. 'I'd love to perform with him or Josh Groban. Andrea Bocelli's first album, *Romanza*, was the very first album I ever bought, when I was about eleven. He has got a really nice voice and manages to put across emotion when he sings. He draws people in to what he is doing. The same goes for Josh Groban. 'I guess I take inspiration from everyone, really, even just from watching people perform on TV, or listening to CDs. Celine Dion has a lovely voice; I love her vocal gymnastics and the strength in her voice. I sang quite a few of her songs when I was younger. She's got a stunning voice and she's also so driven. I've read one of her books and she's an inspiration. And then there's Kate Bush, who is a completely different kind of singer, so talented and unique.'

For inspiration on how to manage her career, Hayley quite naturally cites the example of Dame Kiri Te Kanawa. 'Apart from her fantastic voice, there's the fact she's from New Zealand and had international success. It shows people that even coming from a small country like New Zealand you can still make it overseas.'

Another international success story who has provided both inspiration and practical assistance to Hayley has been Christchurch-based Dame Malvina Major. Her partner, Brian Law, had conducted the Sky City Starlight Symphony concert in Auckland at which Hayley sang – of course – 'Pie Jesu'. It was one of the first times she had performed with a proper opera microphone, and the voice sounded even clearer and truer than usual in the night air. Law was impressed. He asked if Hayley had ever sung for Major, and told Jill to call him when the family got back to Christchurch. As soon as they did so, Jill walked into the house and said, 'I just have to ring someone.'

'You *did* ring straight away, didn't you,' said Law when he answered the phone.

'He came home and said he had heard this young girl and he thought I should hear her because she just needed a few things,' says Major. 'Then she came and had an audition with me and it started there.'

When Major agreed to coach the youngster, it was a one-in-a-million opportunity for Hayley to get the benefit not only of the seasoned soprano's technical knowledge but also of her career experience. More than anyone Hayley had encountered so far, Major was qualified to assess and guide her voice at a critical point in its development.

'My first reaction was that it was a very true and honest and pretty voice, though not a big voice,' sums up Major. 'What was rare was that she sang unaccompanied a lot of the time and never went off. It's easier to stay true if you have accompaniment. Her ability to stay pure and keep the tone and colours is something you are either born with or not.

'When I heard her, I told her what I felt she needed more than anything, because she was so young, was breathing technique and the ability to support the voice as it grows. Also her diction was pretty bad. That's clicked in now.'

Major was teaching at Canterbury University but made time to give Hayley the occasional lesson after school. Both parties had numerous other commitments, and time had to be seized where it could. 'She could teach a lot in a quarter of an hour,' says Hayley. 'When I could get a lesson with her, it was great.'

Hayley was just as good a pupil for Major as she was for her teachers at Burnside High School. Like them, Major noted the youngster's determination to get things right. Hayley taped all her lessons, and if she didn't understand anything always asked for an explanation. Sophie and Isaac were usually there too, and Major noted that Hayley's sister was also particularly attentive to what she was saying.

Major concentrated on the technical aspects of Hayley's voice. 'She needed to know how to breathe, to be aware of what her diaphragm did and to develop the lungs. She had a very slight frame, and I made her aware of how the body will support the voice. If you don't attend to that, the voice and jaw get a judder. She was very quickly into that. We concentrated also on quite high singing because that's where her natural voice was.

'Once the breathing kicks in, the voice develops a larger resonance. The whole range of her voice, but especially the top, grew in strength from the breathing. At that age, the voice will grow like the body, but you need to guide it along. I know when she is eighteen or nineteen she'll reap the benefit of what we were doing.'

Major gave Hayley songs that stretched her, but not too far. When Hayley asked if she could sing a couple of opera numbers, she was refused.

So much for the voice. What could Major tell Hayley to help her with her career? The direction was still to be decided. Major 'was a bit unsure about opera, because the voice is not very big. She was right for musical theatre before she chose crossover. If that had been the way she ended up going, I would have encouraged movement classes as well. I think she should still do dancing along with what she's doing now. She might need to have that in the future.'

Brian Law had also emphasised to Hayley that a good voice alone was not enough on which to build a career. He advised her to continue studying dancing and acting to make herself a total performer.

And there was advice on details, such as not leaving all her learning until the last minute if she had a big performance coming up, like a schoolgirl cramming for an examination.

Like everyone else who came in contact with them, Major also developed an interest in the Westenra family. When it became clear that Hayley would need to spend a lot of time overseas and Jill was unsure how to organise things with the younger children, Major, who has three children of her own, advised her to take them too.

CHAPTER FIVE

Hayley's Gift

Before work was begun on *My Gift to You*, Hayley's second album for Universal, the company's head, George Ash, who believed Hayley had what it took to succeed internationally, had brought her to the attention of sister company Decca in the UK. Decca had respect for the New Zealand management, because this country had done well with some of their artists, notably tenor Russell Watson.

But, much as Hayley's demo had sat unheard in Auckland record company offices before finally coming to anyone's attention, so too it languished for some time on a desk in London before being heard by another crucial figure in Hayley's career, Costa Pilavachi, president of the Decca Music Group.

Pilavachi, who coincidentally had worked with Brian Law in Ottawa, is a significant figure in the contemporary classical music business. An urbane, peripatetic Greek, he understands music, food, wine and what is needed for the classical music industry to survive. And part of that is crossover.

'A couple of colleagues had said, "We got this from a young girl in New Zealand,"' says Pilavachi. 'I looked at it and thought, Charlotte Church covers. I wasn't sure the world was ready for another fourteen-year-old wunderkind.'

Pilavachi put the material to one side without listening to it and went on to other things. 'Then a couple of weeks later I was walking upstairs in the marketing department, and I heard this female voice singing the first track I ever heard Bocelli sing, which sold me on him: "Il Mare Calmo Della Sera".

'I stopped dead in my tracks. I had no idea who it was, but I thought it was unbelievable – the phrasing, the quality of sound, she captured the essence of the song perfectly. I was just blown away.'

Pilavachi realised it was the voice of the girl he had shown no interest in before, and berated his staff for not forcing him to listen to it. 'They said, "You were in a bad humour, and you were right. Who can possibly be into another girl like this?" Everyone was pessimistic, but I said, "The voice is unbelievable."'

After discussing Hayley with George Ash in Auckland, Pilavachi saw a video of her on *60 Minutes*. 'I saw this attractive, healthy young family, and I thought what we should do is take a different approach [from that taken with Charlotte Church] so we don't look like copycats. We thought about having a family act. We brainstormed that with George for a while.'

In whatever way Decca would finally decide to market Hayley, Pilavachi knew he had to meet her and her family to see if they had the stamina and will to cope with the demands that would be put upon them if Hayley was to have an international career. He arranged to fly to New Zealand.

Adam Holt had taken over from George Ash at Universal by the time Pilavachi arrived in August 2001. He recalls, 'I came in and I just got given a name: "Costa is interested in her." I didn't know who Costa was. I'd been in the seat one day. It took about three or four months to set him up. He was passionate enough to come down.'

Holt understood Pilavachi's vision for shepherding Decca through the decline in the core classical music industry. He had championed artists like Watson and the female quartet Bond, the 'classical Spice Girls' (a label that sits as comfortably with them as the 'new Charlotte Church' did with Hayley). Hayley was a natural fit with this process, and her timing could not have been better.

One anecdote sums up Pilavachi's pragmatic philosophy. 'We were in a taxi,' Holt recalls, 'and there was a review on National Radio of Bond, slagging it off. Costa started laughing. "They just don't get it," he said. "I've sold 400,000 of these." That's what it's about. He understands the commercial nature of it.'

Pilavachi spent his first day in Auckland being briefed by Adam Holt before travelling with him to Wellington, where Hayley was scheduled to sing at a corporate function. There was no time to meet Hayley before the concert, though she was well aware that a man who could change her and her family's life would be out there somewhere in the audience, listening and judging.

Despite the pedestrian context, it was to be a 'star-is-born' moment. 'It was full of older gentlemen,' says Pilavachi, 'and a rather provincial-looking audience. The whole thing was tacky but fun. We were sitting in the balcony. A portly gentleman in a lime-green blazer introduced Hayley. I had never set eyes on her until then. She came out on this drab stage and I remember my colleague and I looking at each other, nodding and saying, "She's a star." She sang beautifully. That was it.'

'Hayley came out and cut through really well,' says Adam Holt. 'When I looked at Costa he was beaming. She came back after a few awards had been given out. The crowd was a bit rowdy by now, but she just cut through it. I looked around and Costa's got his hands in the air going: "Yes, yes! She's a star, she's a star!" He kept saying her voice was like a bell.'

Pilavachi and Holt went back to her hotel to meet Hayley and Jill, who had accompanied her, after the show. But many of the audience were also staying at the hotel, and were equally keen to meet the young singer and join in the chorus of praise. The executives managed a brief chat, but anything more would have to wait until the next day when they visited the family at home in Christchurch. Pilavachi was already sold. The rest was confirmation and detail.

The whole Westenra family was apprehensive about the visit of the high-flying music industry figure. 'There was a bit of a panic because we knew he was coming to our house,' says Hayley. 'And then it was a bit nerve-wracking knowing he'd make the final decision and decide whether or not I was suitable for this contract. And we didn't know what he was looking for.'

Jill was worried the family would not measure up. When they went to lunch together, she was relieved that the waiter could speak with authority on wine. 'It was a very positive experience,' she recalls. 'I didn't cringe at any point. When we drove to our house we had to take a corporate cab, and Hayley's going, "This is really flash." I was thinking Costa had probably flown business class and it was really upmarket and then it was like . . . here's our house. He didn't mind.

'He was just observing a lot of the time. He didn't say a lot. It wasn't tense, but we were very aware that he was observing, though we didn't know quite what. And you knew it was important, but there was nothing you could do except do your best to be nice and chat away.'

Hayley appreciated that Pilavachi was 'really nice to Isaac and Sophie as well. He was into the whole family travelling together and all that.'

For his part, Pilavachi, like many before and after him, soon fell under the spell of the family's warmth and sincerity.

More than anything, the visit was proof that the great big international record company was not going to take the tiny ingenue and proceed to squeeze every dollar out of her they could. It is an attitude that has mutual benefits: Jill and Gerald Westenra get to preserve their family while seeing their daughter succeed, and the record company gets a stable artist who will be able to sustain a long-term career.

The next step was organising the deal. By the time Pilavachi got to Christchurch, a framework was in place. He, Adam Holt and Holt's Australian counterpart Peter Bond had thrashed it out on the plane between Wellington and Christchurch.

'Universal assigned the contract over to Decca,' says Holt. 'Decca took over full responsibility for marketing Hayley globally in return for some benefits to New Zealand which would only be of big value to us if the record was successful. If it wasn't, we wouldn't have got any money. The good thing for us was that for a small company like New Zealand to deliver an artist to the world would have cost us millions. I wouldn't have the skill to market it internationally. If I ring PolyGram Germany and say, "I've got this great artist," they say, "How nice, do send us the CD." But when Decca say, "We're going to be releasing this in March or April 2004," they go, "Please send me the pack and we'll get cracking."

'That deal was the right thing to do for Hayley. It put her in the right environment and took away the business limitations from Universal's point of view; I had no risk and Hayley has benefited.'

Back in London, says Pilavachi, 'Everyone thought I was completely mad. They said, "It's so far, and how can you bring her here?" It seemed so impractical for a London-based label, but she was clearly so special and had made such a sensation in her own country. New Zealand is a very normal place, so I figured it should appeal to people in other countries.'

The contract was for five albums. Interviewed at the time of the deal, Hayley, unsurprisingly, described it as 'cool'.

Dealing with the contract was, for once, something the family could not teach themselves. Instead, respected entertainment lawyer Campbell Smith took care of their interests. According to Smith's observations, Hayley was now very much the entertainment industry veteran in the family. He describes contracts such as the one she had to sign as 'designed to confuse people', but as he went through it clause by clause with

Hayley, Jill and Gerald, he noted that Hayley's ability to focus on what she was reading outlasted Jill's and Gerald's, whose attention span was closer to the norm. While their heads began to spin, Hayley soldiered on. However, she does not share Smith's appraisal of her legal aptitude. 'I was signing this big thick contract,' she says, 'and I'm like, you know, "I'm so glad we don't have to deal with it ourselves."' She dutifully initialled every page 'as though I'd read everything, but I hadn't.'

And she did grasp one important financial detail which is often lost on older performers: she would be paying for everything, because expenses would be deducted from the revenue she generated. 'People think you can just get the record company to pay for everything – they don't understand that you pay for it in the end from your royalties.' It's one reason why her lifestyle is far from extravagant, and why the assumption that she's rolling in money galls.

Malvina Major's observations of the music industry and how someone like Hayley can fit in are worth noting at this stage. 'It was always obvious she had the ability to make a career,' says Major. 'But I never pinned my hopes on anything like that because it depends on how you get picked up [by a label]. Circumstances make a career, and I wasn't sure whether the company or people round her were that serious. She was small and gorgeous but not flamboyant.

'The scary thing for me is seeing kids go into the business, and they get to nineteen or twenty and they're has-beens as far as the record company is concerned. A person must have stamina to go on and face their life and snap out of it. I think Hayley's got that.'

The exact nature of Hayley's first Decca album, which would be recorded in the UK, would take a long time to be decided. One easy, and often used, option would have been to re-record successful numbers from her first two albums. But Pilavachi, and others, were looking for a long-term strategy. He knew she would not be fourteen forever but that, handled properly, she could have a long-term career. The first Decca album would be seen as a sign of things to come. It was a time to start looking forward, not looking back.

But first there would be another album in New Zealand for Universal. And it would be in the making of this that her future direction would start to become clear.

Following the success of *Hayley Westenra*, Universal naturally wanted to produce a follow-up. The first plan was to reissue that disc with some bonus tracks. That developed into a mini-album, which in turn became a full-length release, *My Gift to You* – and there was just time to get it out for the Christmas market. Incredibly, this would be fourteen-year-old Hayley's third CD. It was also the first to be made entirely under Universal's control, even if it would have to be produced in a hurry to meet the deadline.

David Selfe, who had produced *Hayley Westenra*, was brought in again to record what were expected to be four or five tracks. To speed things up, composer and producer Jim Hall came on board to produce the balance of songs to make a complete album.

Hall accompanied Adam Holt to one of Hayley's concerts. He is an easy-going man with experience across a few decades and many kinds of music, from the pop variety show *Happen Inn*, to jazz gigs, to touring with the musical *Godspell*. He met Hayley and Jill and found the chemistry was right.

One of the issues Hall confronted early on was exactly what kind of music Hayley should be singing. He noted, as had Dame Malvina, that she would never be big enough to be an opera singer. Hayley was and is fine with that – she likes opera, but she doesn't love it the way she does other styles. 'The first run of songs we had for *My Gift to You* was incredibly conservative,' says Hall. 'I started doing the album before I'd met her. I did a couple of tracks guessing where her range would be. So it was happening pretty quickly, but I was always trying to get through to her that from now on she had to think more like an originator and less like an imitator.'

Everyone wanted the album to be more than just Christmas songs, in order for it to have a sales life for the rest of the year. Decca were keen to use the album to push Hayley in a more internationally appealing direction than she had been working in so far. But that was the least of Hall's worries.

'I only had about three weeks to do it, and less money for the whole album than one day's orchestra recording would have cost for [Hayley's later album] *Pure*,' says Hall. 'As it turns out, a lot of it is midi [computer]-orchestrated. But there was no option – even if I'd had the money I didn't have the time to put an orchestra in there.' The album was completed in little more than a month.

There was serendipity as well as chaos along the way. Before he'd become involved with the album, Hall and Boh Runga had written a promotional song for a charity and there had been talk of Hayley singing it. The charity deal fell through, but the song, 'All I Have to Give', became the first track on the new disc. By the time it became a possibility for Hayley, it was already orchestrated and ready for her to add vocals to.

Hayley was far more involved in track selection than she had been previously. 'I chose a lot of them,' she says. 'I said no to "Once in Royal David's City".' She also turned 'Away in a Manger' down flat. No one realised it at the time, but the album would also contain one track, included only at Hayley's insistence, that would point the way forward for the rest of her career. That song was 'Mary Did You Know?'.

Despite all the input from the mature professionals, says Hall, this was the most perceptive choice on the album. 'Mary Did You Know?' is quintessential crossover. 'It was a song that, when she knew she was going to do a Christmas album, she had to have,' says Jim Hall. 'That was when I realised Hayley had some balls. She wanted this song. It was one of her favourites. And when Decca heard it they got a bit of a sense of direction.' (It's also the only track on the album recorded using artificial fingernails. Hall plays guitar and had to put on fake nails because he had broken his when fishing.)

'"Mary" was the track on the Christmas album held up as the blueprint for an international record,' agrees Adam Holt. 'I think it also gave Hayley confidence that she knew what she wanted. I always thought she was too polite and would let people push her round. I said, "If you know what you want, you've got to say it."'

Several of the songs that had been chosen for the album by the time Hall got to it he found 'a bit Anglican', especially if it was to appeal to a broader market than Hayley's existing one.

And she was still too young to be singing about the sort of romantic love that is the subject of most popular songs. 'We were thinking of songs from musicals, like "If I Loved You" by Rodgers and Hammerstein. It's a wonderful song but it still didn't seem right that she would be singing about these things.

'This problem will slowly go away over time, but basically you're left with songs about bunnies and children. A couple are nice, but a whole album is tough going. Or they're religious songs, where you can express your love but it's for the Big Guy. So we came to "You'll Never Walk Alone". The minute it was suggested, everyone said, "Yeah." So I did a slightly out-there version, a gospelly take to make it cooler. "Chestnuts Roasting on an Open Fire" is a song I insisted we put on because it's a great American Christmas song that doesn't get heard much in New Zealand. And also it was a little bit jazzy and different from the kind of stuff she was doing.'

My Gift to You was also the first album on which Hayley sang songs that hadn't previously been recorded by other artists. Without an existing model to base a performance on – or against – she faced a new challenge to which she rose with her trademark intelligence and determination.

She was given demos to get an idea of how the songs could sound, but Hall didn't want her imitating anyone or agonising over her performances. 'I just wanted her to come in and sing. I believe the first performance is quite often the best, and I hate spending hours and hours on a song. Especially with someone like her, who's never out of tune. Hayley is a one-take wonder.'

Another track has become one of Hayley's signature tunes. Although it has been recorded time and again by New Zealand and overseas artists, she has managed to put her own stamp on 'Pokarekare Ana'. Jim Hall was an old hand at 'Pokare', having produced a popular version that was used in a widely seen TV commercial. He added some synthesisers and adapted this into even more of a crossover style for Hayley.

The production of 'Over the Rainbow' was a little more complicated. Hayley was a fan of the Eva Cassidy version, which is sung in double time but at half the speed, 'and the song takes twice as long to get through,' says Hall. 'That leaves you with huge, long notes, especially without an orchestra. I got the idea of doing it with a Neapolitan orchestra, so grabbed my trusty mandolin and played all the orchestral parts on that.'

One of the last songs to be chosen was 'Morning Has Broken'. There was little time left to agonise over choices, and the Cat Stevens song was one that Hayley already knew well. 'It was getting near to the time I had to deliver the album,' Hall remembers, 'and I thought it was looking a little bit boring. There was nothing populist in there. We were tossing songs around, and Hayley liked this one when it came up.' Somewhat hurriedly, and in reversal of the normal order, Hayley delivered a perfect rendition of 'Morning Has Broken' and Hall put a backing behind it later.

For two tracks, 'Do You Hear What I Hear?' and 'Through These Eyes', Hayley was joined on vocals by her old busking partner, Sophie Westenra, aged eleven.

'Considering the incredible deadline, I don't know why I took it on, but I'm glad I did. If we'd had more time we'd have made it better,' says Hall. 'It was an exercise in terror, but we got there.'

Looking back, Hall says Hayley was the only person who remained calm throughout the production. Told this, Hayley says drily, 'Maybe I just contained my little uncertainties and concerns.'

As for Jill, who accompanied Hayley to the sessions, she found the process very different from the way they had been used to working. 'I was so used to the idea you needed time to learn songs properly. I wanted it to be the best Hayley could do, and was a bit worried she wouldn't have time to prepare.' But once she realised that Hall was a pro who knew what he was doing, Jill relaxed.

Hayley learned a lot from her two albums with Universal, and Universal learned a lot from Hayley too. 'The biggest thing I learned,' says Adam Holt, 'is that you can get really caught up in hip A&R – the bands everyone's raving about. Hayley is not the "coolest" girl in the world, but she can sell more records than anyone had for a long time. She taught me that successful records come in all sorts of shapes and sizes. You have to look for true talent and it will shine through if you pitch it right and the timing is right.'

The next album, her first for Decca, would be recorded overseas. It would have to perform numerous functions, not least justifying Costa Pilavachi's faith in the girl from half a world away. Fortunately, it would be pitched right and timed right.

CHAPTER SIX

Cause Without a Rebel

Almost from the time she became known as a singer Hayley has been asked repeatedly when she is going to rebel. The unspoken inference behind these questions is that she has been railroaded into a life not entirely of her own choosing, whether by her parents or her record company.

Jill and Gerald both labour under a common public misconception that they are 'stage parents' – a label that carries a range of negative connotations. Such a belief fails to credit Hayley with the strength of will she has demonstrated time and again. 'It's not possible to pressure kids into doing what Hayley's doing,' says one family friend. 'Jill and Gerald have gone with the flow. You see people who do push their kids, and the kids aren't happy. Hayley is so well balanced.'

There is a lengthy roll of observers who know both the Westenras and show business better than any outsider and who dispute the stage-parents criticism.

'She definitely hasn't been pushed by her parents,' says Malvina Major, who gave her own children the opportunity to perform but respected their decisions to go into other areas. 'The mother has possibly gone that one step further than a lot of mothers – but I don't think she was the typical pushy sort. She was amazed when it took off.'

It is the family's friends who often hear – and have to defend – the criticism, as few people will say anything directly to Jill and Gerald. Martine Carter has known Hayley longer, and more intimately, than most. 'Hayley has been the one who wanted to do it,' she says. 'Isaac has said he doesn't want to do things sometimes, and Jill knows there's no point pushing them into things they're not interested in. But she has carried them along once they've got into an interest. I would have thought it was all too much to do long ago.'

Hayley concurs. She told one interviewer she thinks that even now her parents would be quietly relieved if she gave up.

Director Richard Jay Alexander, who worked with Hayley on Russell Watson's Auckland Domain concert in February 2002, has seen one extreme of the stage-parent phenomenon up close. 'You're talking to an American who understands the monstrous showbiz parent,' he says. 'That's not the case with Hayley. She's a normal kid. I always have to meet the parents, because you want to know who's doing the driving – the child or the parents. There's plenty of the latter out there, and some have started hitting the reality shows.'

It's not just Americans who see this sort of parenting. 'I've met some kids with their parents,' says Christchurch Symphony's business development manager Steve Brooker, 'and the parents are pushing them like mad. There's none of that with the Westenras. It's all completely natural.'

It just happened that Jill's attitude to parenting was conducive to producing a sane, well-balanced performer. 'When I had wee children,' she says, 'I was just proud of my gorgeous children. I didn't need to think of them on stage.' For her it's about doing what you do well – it doesn't matter what it is. 'You can pick the children with pushy parents because they're almost reluctantly up there. You can see in their faces they're only doing it for mum. And they could be doing something else they're really good at.'

The last word on the subject should probably go to Hayley's teacher Lois Butler: 'No one who knows the family criticises them.'

The stage-parents accusation looks plausible from the outside, but if there is any railroading going on, the evidence shows it to be in the opposite direction. By the time Hayley was sixteen, she had already taken on and beaten her record company in one major battle, as we shall hear later, and even she acknowledges that her parents' lives might be a little easier if she were not so driven.

In the film *The Wild One*, when asked what he is rebelling against, motorbike bad boy Johnny says, 'What have you got?' Hayley's attitude to the issues is the reverse: what could she possibly want to rebel against? She does, however, reserve the right to change her mind later.

'I guess this is my rebelling age,' she says, 'but I don't feel the need to rebel against anything. I guess it's seeing pictures of Charlotte Church smoking and wanting to go into pop that makes people ask me about it. But I'm happy with what I'm doing. It's not like my parents are annoying me or I'm doing something I don't want to be doing. I'm happy here where I am. But you never know . . .'

'I think every step of the way, this is what she wanted,' says Jill, who sometimes has to apply the brakes to the runaway Hayley train. 'She's been the driving force in her own career. I'm worried about her health, scared she'll get sick. I schedule in rest time, days off, but something will come up and she'll say, "But I really want to do this." So it's her choice. What would she be rebelling against? She'd be rebelling against herself.

'I remember in Auckland, on the waterfront, when she'd just got the Universal contract, and I said, "Do you really want this?" It was just one of those brief moments where you think, Maybe this is all going too fast. She said, "Don't be so silly. Of course I do."'

'They get exhausted but Hayley loves it,' says one family friend of the hectic pace of Westenra life. 'I've heard Jill say it won't be that long before Hayley is out on her own. They're there for her now when she needs them, and when she's old enough to do her own thing they'll let her.'

And that will spare Hayley the fate of Charlotte Church, whose high public profile and angelic early image meant her normal teenage behaviours – a cigarette! a tattoo! a boyfriend! – were magnified to make her look like the most rebellious individual since Spartacus.

Church has been a presence in Hayley's life for a long time. Jill would watch Church's career from afar and wonder how someone so young could have achieved so much, never suspecting that her daughter would one day surpass her achievements.

'I found her to be far superior to Charlotte Church,' enthuses Richard Jay Alexander. 'I know it's not a bake-off, and Charlotte Church has her own career, but the issue for me is about clarity of instruments. I find Hayley's instrument so pure, so clear. For me Charlotte Church's voice is in the middle of the throat. It doesn't have the soaring power.'

Not the least of Hayley's talents is that of never saying the wrong thing. Her comments about Charlotte Church have always been tactful and respectful, even as the comparison grew increasingly irritating and irrelevant. Asked once if she could see a future team of Three Sopranos, comprising herself, Church and sister Sophie, she patiently said, 'I think Charlotte Church has done really well and she should be very proud of what she has achieved. I'm not trying to be the next Charlotte Church – I'm just doing what I really enjoy. I think it would be really cool for us all to sing together and I know Sophie would love it, but it's probably very unlikely.'

'Hayley respects Charlotte Church,' says Steve Abbott, who has been Hayley's manager since 2003. 'But for Hayley, looking at Charlotte Church, it's not a case of, well, that could happen to her, but of, well, that happens.'

The comparisons would dwindle to a trickle in the wake of *Pure*'s success. In the UK, says Hayley, interviewers 'always say, "I know [the comparison is] always brought up at every interview but I'm going to bring it up anyway." People do respect that I'm different and have my own style. There's still the comparison, because to the general public it's the same genre, and we're a similar age, so it seems obvious.'

When Hayley was performing in the UK to promote *Pure*, the had-to-happen-sooner-or-later meeting took place in Cardiff, where she was performing with Russell Watson. Watson's manager knew Church was in the audience, and told Jill. The two didn't let on to Hayley until after the performance. Hayley had just come offstage and was clutching the bunch of flowers with which Watson always presented her at the end of a show when Jill told her.

Church wanted to meet Hayley, and the two spent some time together in a bar at her hotel. 'I remember sitting down and seeing her and going, "Gosh, it's her,"' says Hayley. 'It was weird, because she is the same age as me, but she is the one I've always been compared to. She was really lovely, but it was a little bit tense. You don't know what she's thinking.'

Competitiveness from – and with – other performers is part of Hayley's life now. 'You do sense it sometimes from other performers. It's a competitive market,' she says. She tells of once having to share a dressing room with another crossover act. *Pure* was breaking sales records by the day, and the atmosphere was icy, as the group submitted to the attentions of stylist and make-up artist while Hayley's dad helped her get ready. But when Hayley says, 'It was probably disappointing for them that someone was doing better,' it is with genuine fellow feeling and not a hint of archness.

Hayley's voice is not the only talent she was apparently born with. She has a down-to-earth attitude to work, music and success that many would do well to emulate. It not only makes it possible for her to achieve, it makes others want to help her achieve. As composer Ronan Hardiman, who worked on *Pure*, noted, many people at her level of success expect to be treated differently. They 'suddenly stop doing stairs'. Not Hayley, who still does 'helping people with their luggage' and makes snacks for reporters who visit her at the family home.

Little things mean a lot to Hayley and always have. When Alan Traill wanted to pay her a small tribute after getting to know her through his involvement with McDonald's Young Entertainers, he had a card made for her that read 'VIP Hayley Westenra', entitling her and a friend to free meals at any of his McDonald's restaurants. She loved it.

Gray Bartlett pinpoints another vital element of Hayley's character. 'She has a steely determination,' says the veteran who has seen many successful performers up close over the decades. 'I haven't met anyone else like it. You can tell her to hold a note for five seconds, and she does it with a smile. It's something you can't train people to do. It's got to be in you. Together with that angelic face, it's an incredible combination.

'Sunny is another word that comes to mind. Once we were in the studio doing some demos, and the heat was intense, but she was never fazed. It's obvious she's doing what she wants and her goal is clear.'

It's part of a perfectionism she developed at school. 'She was always very, very meticulous in any written work,' says piano teacher Janie Seed. 'And very apologetic if she didn't get done what she was supposed to.' Then, as now, Hayley hated letting down anyone – especially herself.

Shirley Ireland, Hayley's grandmother, says Hayley has been in charge ever since she began performing. She recounts going to hear her at a shopping centre where the organisation was less than it should have been. 'She was going around saying, "Dad, give me this," and "This goes there." She takes everything in her stride. Nothing throws her.'

She is always prepared to go the extra mile. She has a gift for languages, and when touring non-English-speaking countries she always makes a point of learning at least a few phrases in the local tongue.

'I've got some French and German from school,' says Hayley. 'But when I go to Japan, Malaysia, Hong Kong, I learn a few things, even if I sometimes get them confused. I can usually say, "Hello, I'm Hayley Westenra," and if they write it out phonetically I can do radio station IDs: "Hi, I'm Hayley Westenra and you're listening to radio station whatever."'

All these qualities have helped speed up Hayley's success. Where other artists might have had to learn them, she hit the ground running. Ronan Hardiman, who is best known for composing *Lord of the Dance* for Michael Flatley, knew Hayley had what it took the moment he laid eyes on her.

'She had the whole package,' he says. 'I knew she had been a big success in New Zealand, but she had absolutely no pretensions. She was grounded, calm, personable and open to new ideas. It was very refreshing.' Hardiman renewed his acquaintance with Hayley after the success of *Pure* backstage at a Royal Albert Hall concert and found 'exactly the same person who came into my house two years before.'

Everyone who has encountered Hayley professionally

credits her family with keeping her feet on the ground. Coming from Christchurch has helped too. 'In America,' says Richard Jay Alexander, who has cut his diva teeth on the likes of Barbra Streisand and Bette Midler, 'there's a different kind of privilege belief. There's too much pop culture out there. There's a lot of kids who just want to be stars but they're not expressing anything that has to do with talent or growth or training – they just want the stuff.

'Anyone can grow into a diva but I don't see any signs in Hayley. Also, New Zealand is a gentle country. In America and Americans there's an aggression that's not always welcome around the globe. People get hungry for fame and I don't see that in Hayley. That New Zealand gentleness can be very powerful.'

And by that Alexander means there is something about Hayley that makes people want her to succeed and encourages them to help her.

'And also she's truly beautiful – her skin, her arms, her body language. She's delicate but strong. And she's elegant. She's got a lot of poise for her age and I don't think you can teach that. You can help people learn things, but they either own a stage when they walk out there or they don't. She commands attention, and that's a gift.'

Working with her on *My Gift to You*, Jim Hall found Hayley unusually composed and mature. 'She absolutely listened to what you said, but she also had an opinion and expressed it. She isn't taking in the celebrity bullshit thing at all. I'm a terribly cynical bastard, and I deal with a lot of overblown reputations, but Hayley is a star, in the best possible way. Stars are people you just can't take your eyes off – and that's what Hayley has.'

Hayley was a star in New Zealand with her first three modestly produced albums. To become an international star would require a completely different level of expertise, thought and time.

To ensure her longevity, Decca needed to position Hayley not as a teen prodigy, but as a great voice. You can't be a teenage sensation once you turn twenty. At the same time, she *was* a teen prodigy, and that didn't hurt.

While those around her were pondering just what to do, Hayley continued working as hard as ever. In February 2002 she took part in a performance which would be a career landmark. She was invited to appear with fellow Decca artist and established star Russell Watson at an open-air concert in Auckland's Domain. It would help, in the words of Universal's Alister Cain, to put her on the international radar.

The concert was filmed on a clear Auckland summer night before a huge crowd. It was Hayley's most important performance yet, but as Adam Holt noted, Hayley was 'as cool as a cucumber' (cucumbers could, in fact, take lessons in coolness from Hayley). She sang several numbers, including a duet of 'Pokarekare Ana' with Watson. The pairing was so successful that Hayley was invited to appear with Watson for six concerts of his upcoming UK tour, increasing her exposure even more and giving her a valuable entrée to the UK performing circuit.

No one was more impressed with the Auckland performance than Richard Jay Alexander. 'I remember when she and Russell met onstage,' says Alexander. 'They were both so shy about saying hello. Russell is a big, confident guy and I watched him become boyish around Hayley. It was a very sweet moment.'

Hayley was in the midst of what would become a standard level of hectic activity. She had been performing in New Zealand and Taiwan throughout January, and got back to Auckland in just enough time to be hurried straight to rehearsals, which were being covered by the *Holmes* TV show. Hayley and Russell's first meeting actually took place there, on stage before the cameras. Hayley said later she felt unwell that day, but agreed to sing for the cameras because 'they obviously wanted to hear something, so I gave them what they wanted'.

But there was no sign of strain in her voice then, or during the performance the following night, or on any of her performances with Watson not long after in the UK.

These UK dates were fitted around the recording of the first *Pure* sessions in Dublin and Hayley won over audiences quickly everywhere she went.

There were, however, some cultural niceties to adjust to. One of these was her ignorance of UK football traditions. She was taken aback half an hour before the Newcastle concert when she discovered that 'You'll Never Walk Alone', her show-stopping Rodgers and Hammerstein standard, was soccer rivals' Liverpool's anthem. With mature grace she apologised to the audience for the gaffe before starting to an instant round of applause.

The tour also marked the only time Hayley and her mother have sung on stage together in the UK. On the last show of the tour, in Glasgow, Watson decided he wanted to sing 'Mustang

Sally', which meant he needed backing singers. He had Hayley and his other guest performer, Faye Tozer, on hand, plus a couple of other ring-ins. Somehow, Jill was also dragooned. 'She loved it,' says Hayley.

Jill was reminded of the first time she joined Hayley on stage, to say a few words at a charity concert in Auckland. Seeing the performance from her daughter's point of view, her greatest impression was of . . . fog. She recalls: 'Hayley said, "That's you," and just gave me a little shove. I almost tripped on to the stage. I don't know what I said, but what I noticed is it's all foggy – bright, glary fog, and that's what Hayley's looking out on all the time.'

Although Hayley has no need of publicity gimmicks to attract attention, she unselfconsciously did something on this tour that made headlines around the world. She said 'No' to former Spice Girl Victoria Beckham.

After performing with Watson at London's Wembley Stadium, she was introduced backstage to Victoria's parents, who were there on tickets meant for Victoria and footballer husband David. 'The mother told me she'd rung Victoria on her mobile halfway through when I was singing,' says Hayley. Even over the phone, Victoria liked what she heard enough to invite Hayley to perform at a party for Victoria's birthday.

'They were really keen,' says Hayley. 'They were saying, "You can have anything you want." I was keen to perform as well, except I realised I had to be back in New Zealand for a concert in Auckland and had to attend the New Zealand Music Awards. Also, Sophie was coming up to sing with me at the Auckland concert, so that was a really big deal.

'It was a tough decision,' says Hayley, 'but the thought of cancelling something in New Zealand for a party didn't gel with me, even though when I got back everyone was like, "Why didn't you go to the party?" You can't win.'

It was lucky for the Queen that Hayley didn't have anything planned for the evening she needed to entertain President Bush.

There have been other offers reluctantly declined, and the circumstances get no less strange. Hayley had to pass up an opportunity to switch on the Christmas lights in Moscow because of a scheduling problem. And in early 2004 the World Bank was enthusiastic to have her perform at a special event at the palace of Versailles outside Paris. Unfortunately it clashed with other performance dates. 'They kept on putting up the price, but we just couldn't do it,' says Hayley. 'Even though I want to do extra gigs and the income's good, it's better putting your time and effort into the gigs that will make a difference in the long term rather than chasing the money. It can be annoying sometimes, but you have to be focused, then later you can pick and choose.'

Until she's in the happy position where her record company has recouped its expenses and starts owing her money, high-profile gigs like that for the World Bank are one of the few ways Hayley has of making serious money.

As far as her image went, the Beckham affair did Hayley no end of good. She became the girl who turned down Posh Spice to honour a previous commitment. It was no surprise to those who knew her, but to those who didn't it said that the relatively unknown girl was a person of integrity and honour, whose word meant more to her than dollars.

'It just made sense really,' sums up Hayley. 'There were all these people back home relying on me.'

The association with Watson also led to Hayley's Carnegie Hall début, which was squeezed in around this time, on 1 June 2002. If Hayley was surprised to be preparing to sing at Carnegie Hall at the age of fifteen, others found it unbelievable.

'We had about four days in New York,' says Hayley. 'We went round Times Square and got talking to this old lady. And when we told her I was singing at Carnegie Hall, she was, "Oh no, dear, you must mean the recital hall next door." She just didn't believe me. Then she wanted to know the name of the concert and she was going to check it out.'

By now, *60 Minutes* was Hayley's current affairs show of record, and a crew accompanied the Westenras on this trip to film the event. Someone from the programme treated her to a ride through Central Park in a horse and cart, 'and the driver said a couple of years prior he'd taken Charlotte Church for a ride in the same cart'.

Hayley also found time to brush up on an old skill. 'We thought, Let's do some busking, and did in Times Square. It was for *60 Minutes* as well. But people stopped and they were curious. We thought everyone busked in Times Square. I don't even know if we were allowed to.'

Richard Jay Alexander recalls watching Hayley at rehearsal and being reminded again that this was a family affair. 'You look and understand what it means and it's a momentous event for the family. It's not for Hayley, it's for the family. Allowing their child to follow the dream seems very healthy to me.'

Hayley had to choose a solo number for the concert and was leaning towards 'Who Painted the Moon Black?', the lilting number that would eventually become one of the standouts on *Pure*. Back then, it was unknown. Richard Jay Alexander's opinion was that 'nice as it was, it didn't feel like the slam dunk I thought she needed for her Carnegie Hall début'. He gently suggested that because it was the year of the Richard Rodgers centenary she sing 'You'll Never Walk Alone', which he had heard her perform in New Zealand. The birthday tribute brought the house down.

The concert was also notable for one technical disaster – the sort of thing that Hayley had learned how to deal with in her shopping-mall days but wasn't expecting to confront in Carnegie Hall. Just as she began to sing, feedback hissed through the auditorium. It grew louder and louder as she went on. The sound technicians were slow to react, but Hayley forged ahead.

'First I thought, Oh, I better move my mike away, but it wasn't me. You just carry on. There's no point in making it worse.'

Jill was mildly appalled: 'You think at Carnegie Hall everything should be perfect.' But Alexander had already observed how calmly Hayley was handling matters. As he says, making a Carnegie Hall début at Hayley's age, a lot of people 'would have been hysterical'.

Hayley admits she gets a kick out of being able to say she sang at Carnegie Hall, but says she never forgets that any concert is not about the venue but about the people she is singing to.

CHAPTER SEVEN

Unheard Melody

The biggest thing facing Hayley in 2002 was the recording of *Pure*. For much of that year, she would be making an album that no one would get to hear – a version of *Pure* that would ultimately be abandoned. She knew from the start that the album would be recorded overseas, but exactly what the repertoire was remained fluid. (One of the few stipulations was that Hayley could not sing anything Charlotte Church had recorded.) Songs would frequently land in MP3 form on the Westenras' home computer, and Hayley was initially surprised to learn that some of them were being written especially for her.

International producer Chris Neil was put in charge. He is renowned as a voice specialist, having worked with artists from Rod Stewart to Celine Dion. He had been brought to Auckland with his wife to hear and assess Hayley at the Russell Watson Auckland Domain concert.

Many people were involved in the planning and decisions for the new album. Decca did not simply take over Hayley from Universal once she was signed to them. The New Zealand company was heavily involved with *Pure* in the initial stages.

'Decca were wonderful to us,' says Adam Holt. 'Even though the risk was theirs, they kept us as partners. There was a lot of discussion about what the record would be. More folky? This song? That song? Everyone had an opinion. So they got Chris Neil, who's a really lovely guy.'

'Everything was right about Chris Neil,' says Costa Pilavachi. 'He had worked with greats like Celine Dion. He came to New Zealand and spent time bonding with the family.'

It was through Neil that the Irish composer Ronan Hardiman came aboard. He had heard of Hayley (although she had not yet heard of him), and he became involved in writing and recording for the album.

Hardiman has a studio at his home in Dublin, and it was there that the first sessions took place in April 2002. Hayley and Jill stayed in a nearby hotel, and were joined later by the rest of the Westenras. Hardiman had children of his own and the two families got on well. 'When Hayley wasn't recording,' says Hardiman, 'she'd be helping my daughter with her homework or playing on the trampoline.'

Jill was put at ease by the normalcy of it all, especially on one occasion she remembers vividly, when Ronan's son Sam kept putting his foot on the table despite repeated instructions to the contrary. She was comforted to know that world-class composers had the same issues with their children that everyone else did. Between sessions there was plenty of eating out to enjoy and the odd drop of Guinness.

One day, Hayley became a household name in Hardiman's street. 'We have a monitor at the front of the house so we can see from all the rooms,' relates Hardiman. 'When I'm recording we turn off all the phones. This day, I didn't realise I had left the monitor on, so what was happening in the studio could be heard in the street. When we'd finished, I went out my front door and there was a small crowd of people who'd heard what was happening and just stopped and listened.'

One of the tracks recorded was Hardiman's composition 'Heaven'. Its history is a good example of the up-and-down life a song can have, and the advisability of never throwing anything away because it might come in handy later. 'Heaven' was a semi-instrumental piece on Hardiman's first solo album, *Solace*. With a vocal chorus it became a Top 10 hit in France, which led Hardiman to think it might have even bigger potential. He asked lyricist Frank Musker, who has written for Queen and Ricky Martin, to provide words, and, re-arranged and re-recorded, it would become a highlight of the released *Pure*.

In the studio Hardiman quickly developed enormous respect for Hayley's artistry and professionalism. He was struck by the maturity of her interpretations and her dedication.

'I was very aware of how she was committed to getting the best out of her voice,' he says. 'One evening we were all tired and she was not getting quite what she wanted, so we decided to stop. The next morning we drove to her hotel and she just handed me a note saying she wasn't going to talk. She wanted to preserve her voice because she was determined to nail that note.'

'It was a song that didn't end up on *Pure*, but will be on the next album because I love it,' says Hayley. 'It's "Ave Maria" with English lyrics. It had some really low notes. I had to go in without warming my voice to sing these low notes, so I couldn't say anything. I went down to breakfast and people must have thought, What on earth is going on?' Hayley managed to communicate her breakfast order without words and, says Hardiman, 'Sure enough, when it was time to sing she got it.'

Although the experience of recording was pleasant in every respect, the results were less than satisfactory.

'Hayley had a great rapport with Chris,' says Costa Pilavachi, 'and everything was fantastic, but for some reason – and I still don't understand why – we just never seemed to come together on one thing, and that was how the album should sound.

'All of us at Decca and the Westenras felt it had to have classical elements. And it needed an orchestra – not a full operatic type, but enough to be a classical crossover record, not a pop record. Maybe Chris was so rooted to what he'd done with pop singers, where the producer is in control of the sound completely and it's all created in the studio.' Neil was using electronic backings. 'We didn't feel the setting was the right one. And we had so many meetings but could never come together.'

'We heard some of it,' says Adam Holt. 'It wasn't good. Costa eventually said we needed to redo it. At great cost. We'd been hoping for an album, and then it was delayed. We had to renegotiate our agreement with Decca because naturally the cost went up.'

Holt had other concerns too. 'I was a little nervous. There's a bad second album syndrome in New Zealand where the second albums sell just a fraction of the first.'

'Quite a few gorgeous songs came up that we didn't get to use,' says Hayley, 'but I know we'll put them on the next album.'

Jim Hall had also submitted material for the album, including a clever version of Elgar's 'Nimrod' variation, to which he and Boh Runga had put words. It got lost in the mild confusion when the decision to scrap the Neil *Pure* was made.

Steve Abbott sums up the original tracks as 'someone else's idea of how to make Hayley commercial'. A version of 'Pokarekare Ana' with a Bo Diddley beat was never going to be a winner.

When Decca finally took the decision to scrap *Pure* Version 1.0, there was some personal awkwardness for the Westenras. They had got on so well with everyone involved, but at the upper reaches of the music industry such a move is not uncommon.

'Usually when this happens it's unpleasant,' says Pilavachi. 'But in this case it was all extremely real and natural and everyone was really honest with each other. And sometimes people just don't agree.

'In the end we agreed to disagree. Chris said, "It's obvious this is what I do," and we had to move on. It was a shock for everybody but in a way it was a blessing, because it gave Hayley and us and the project time to settle and mature rather than rushing a record out within a year. She grew up a little bit, distanced herself from the Charlotte Church thing, travelled more, got to understand better what it means to be a star.

'And Chris Neil has been a complete gentleman. He's delighted with Hayley's success. We've never exchanged the slightest unpleasant word. Just the other day he brought me a

Schumann song he's written words for and demo-ed up the way Hayley would like to hear it.'

Elements of the first *Pure*, after going through some changes, were part of the eventual product. As well as Hardiman's own 'Heaven', several tracks, like the Vivaldi 'River of Dreams' and the Ravel 'Never Say Goodbye' were part of the Chris Neil product. And Ronan Hardiman had discovered the Namibian song, 'Who Painted the Moon Black?'.

Hayley's view? 'It [*Pure*] was a lot poppier than it is now, with lots of drumbeats in the background. It's more New Agey now. I think, looking back, [the production was] a bit too harsh for the music. The recording we did with Chris and Ronan could have done well, but I think I'm happier with the more organic sound.

'But it was a learning curve, and I discovered what I liked. So it wasn't wasting time, but it seemed like it at the time. It's awful when you think you've done something and then find you've got to do it again.

'At times you get caught up in what you're doing and think it's great. But then you can look back and realise it wasn't. I just wanted to release the album, and everyone asked when it was coming out. It wasn't really that long, but at the time it was like an eternity.'

Part of the problem, unavoidably, was that there had never been a Hayley before. There was no one to look to as a model for her kind of music. In fact, it was still unclear just what her kind of music was. With the eventual runaway success of the completed *Pure*, produced by Giles Martin, Hayley herself has become a model to emulate. The Martin product, so meticulously planned and carefully presented, will itself become a template for other crossover performers.

Music critics often deride the contemporary music industry as putting marketing before all other considerations. Those at the coalface would probably agree that, yes, they do see it as part of their job to sell records. But, as Costa Pilavachi says, the record company is a conduit for Hayley's talents. Without people like her, people like him would not have a job. It is therefore crucial that he and the others involved do the best they can to sell as many of Hayley's records as possible. Which means marketing her as well as possible.

The crucial issue of marketing is a chicken and egg one – do you make a recording and then work out how to sell it, or do you work out what will sell, and then make a record to fit?

Hayley's ultimate success involved a little bit of chicken with some egg thrown in. She is not a pop singer, she is not an opera singer, she is not a musical theatre performer. She could have had a stab at all of those, but emerging at this time was the popularity of crossover, which suited her taste, her abilities and her record company's vision. Fortunately, her own not especially eclectic taste was a perfect fit. 'I really enjoy listening to Joni Mitchell, Vanessa Carlton, Alicia Keys, Kate Bush, Nelly Furtado and Alessandro Safina,' she says. 'I prefer singing slightly more classically based songs because they're more suited to my voice and style.'

The first *Pure* was crossover, but, with its artificial backings and drumbeats, probably not crossover enough. The problems with that recording brought to light how important it was to define Hayley's position in the musical spectrum. Like the recording itself, the process was somewhat tortuous, but it provides a fascinating insight into how the contemporary music industry works.

'When we first heard about her,' says marketing director for Universal Classics and Jazz UK, Dickon Stainer, 'we didn't want her to make a classical crossover album. Charlotte Church had done that. But by the time the album was three-quarters finished, time had gone by and we changed our mind. Charlotte Church didn't matter any more. When it came to the final album, we wanted one that was more classical than was first talked about.'

Somehow, Hayley had to be made different from other artists. 'It's like going into a post office queue for letters or parcels,' says Stainer. 'There was no one in the queue she was going in. If she'd gone down the pop route straight away, she'd have got lost. We were very keen to make sure she was in a market all her own.'

Hayley had one advantage over many of her fellow crossover artists. 'She appeals to young people in a way other crossovers, like Russell Watson, don't,' explains Stainer. 'Some young people, especially girls, identify with her. She's straightforward and uncomplicated.'

Richard Jay Alexander is another who understands the process, especially for young performers. 'You can't keep these kids in a cage,' he says. 'They have to grow and people will grow with them, but what does that growth include? Some people have made that deadly mistake in crossover where growth just never continued. I think Hayley has so much possibility.'

Hayley had been aware of, though not forced to confront, the issue for some time. 'The big decision for Hayley,' says Malvina Major, 'was quite a traumatic one, when we all honed in deeply on her about what she wanted to do. An agent friend talked to her and said, "If you want to be an opera singer, give this nonsense away." Then she rang and asked me what I thought. I took about three weeks. I saw not an opera voice, body or person. The easiest thing was to go with what was being offered.'

Gray Bartlett, too, thought Hayley was the perfect crossover artist, and notes that it leaves her room to develop in other directions. 'I saw the crossover thing – pop, Irish, Celtic, the ballady type song – as what she should go for.' He cites the example of Josh Groban, whose recordings each include at least one example of a new style. 'You touch the edges of other things, to see if there's a new market coming. No one stays at the top forever. But she is able now to go in all kinds of directions. Hayley is lucky because she's got a career in films or stage musicals if she wants it.'

For now, Hayley is happy to be described as a crossover artist, although the definition is still evolving. The style has gone through a New Age period, which wasn't entirely congenial, and grown to incorporate other elements, including, as she says, 'a bit of a beat plus the classical aspect'. Another part of the genre's appeal is that 'I feel I can put true emotion into it, whereas some of the operatic songs are harder for me to relate to and aren't really representative of me.'

When recording for *Pure* II started, no one would be in any doubt that they were making a crossover album.

CHAPTER EIGHT

Pure II

Hayley would probably not have found making *Pure* in the alien environment of London as pleasant as she did if her parents had not taken turns being there with her. At one stage the whole family planned to go, but that proved impractical. The family of five did manage to spend six weeks together in the two-bedroom Kensington flat, but for most of the year Jill and Gerald were seldom together and Sophie and Isaac were separated from at least one parent and their sister. It was a major family commitment.

But it was important that somebody was there to make sure Hayley got to sleep at night, that everything was organised for her during the day and, often, to protect her from extra demands on her time.

Hayley, still a student at Burnside High, also wanted to continue with her schoolwork, though that was an aim more honoured in the intention than the achievement. She had hoped to sit the English A Levels, for which she studied extramurally, but organised education frequently gave way to career commitments.

Their first flat was sandwiched between Kensington Gardens and Holland Park. Hayley and Jill did yoga and joined the library. Portobello market was a short walk away, and the gardens were an ideal spot for running to keep up fitness. The two would jog together regularly, never getting over a small sense of wonderment that they were running where Princess Diana used to run and were otherwise in touch with a certain glamorous aura of English life.

They soon learned how to negotiate the bus and tube routes to get around the city. Hayley (and the rest of the family) preferred organic and vegetarian foods, which were easy to obtain from local shops. Drinking water was another matter, but they got used to lugging litres of bottled water back home.

In the second half of the year, during promotional work for *Pure*, they moved to a flat in Covent Garden. 'I enjoyed London,' says Hayley. 'It's probably the closest culture to New Zealand's, and it was very easy to fit in. Where we stayed is a fun place, handy to the tube and shops. It was just an interesting place to be.'

However, there was little time to experience the musical life of the city – something Hayley was happy to defer to quieter times. 'I'd love to go see more movies and watch shows but you just have to be focused,' she says. 'I felt like I experienced some of the London culture just living there. Everyone says, you have to see this or that, and I really wanted to see *Les Misérables* and

Phantom of the Opera. Our flat in Covent Garden was right next to the theatre where *Chicago* was on. We heard the music every night, so I felt I had an invitation to that.

'Travelling's fun to some extent, but you get a little bit homesick, especially when the rest of the family is back home, and you're on the phone finding out what they did at school today and Mum's probably thinking, I wish I was back there with them.'

Hayley's homesickness would only get bad when she was close to returning to Christchurch. At that point Jill would refrain from mentioning home too often because it only exacerbated the problem.

Before work could begin on *Pure* II, the perfect producer had to be employed. But how to find an expert on something that had never been done before?

'We took almost six months to explore other producers and other concepts,' says Costa Pilavachi. 'It was hard to find the right person. They needed a modicum of classical training and crossover experience. There are not that many people who feel comfortable in that area.'

Giles Martin was one such person. He bears the label 'son of Beatles producer Sir George Martin' the way Hayley carries 'new Charlotte Church' – with as much inevitability and as little enthusiasm. By the time he came to *Pure*, his background included stints as a performer with Velvet Jones and as a producer with the group My Life Story. Decca had several meetings with Martin before making their decision. 'He was the first producer who came with a demo that indicated he understood Hayley and her voice,' says Pilavachi.

Also a contender for a while was Sarah Class, a talented arranger, composer and producer who would provide many of the arrangements for *Pure,* and one song, 'Across the Universe of Time'.

'We were torn between Giles and Sarah,' says Pilavachi, 'and said, "Why not both?" So Sarah became the orchestrator, and Giles the producer. It was a risk. There's no one who has a track record in this area. Most of those records that succeed do it by accident.'

'Those two people really shaped the album,' says Hayley. 'Sarah did amazing arrangements. Like "Dark Waltz" – that was one of the songs Chris Neil found. Sarah put this violin solo at the beginning and it sounded so nice. I'm really grateful to Giles and Sarah.'

Steve Abbott, who came on the scene between completion and release of the album, was enormously impressed by Martin and by the way he handled what was always going to be a delicate task. 'I can't speak highly enough of Giles as a person,' says Abbott. 'He had to take control of the album. They'd made it and it got scrapped, so he came into a very awkward situation and didn't have a big track record. He's one of the few people who understands what Hayley wants to do musically, and he connects with her on a personal level.'

Producer and performer were in harmony from the start, though Hayley wasn't overly sure at first. 'The first time we met him was at a café in Portobello Road that Decca organised and we struggled to find,' says Hayley. 'He speaks with a very posh English accent. We gave him this big bone and paua Maori carving. I assume he was thinking, Gosh, what's this? It may not have suited how he likes to present himself.

'Then we had a meeting at our flat, with him, Jacky Schroer from Decca A&R, and Mum and I. Everyone was on the same wavelength.'

To Hayley, the most important thing was that she love each and every song. 'We were finding a balance on key issues, and the biggest one was between classical and pop. The pop songs were popular with all of us, but we had to be careful because we could blow it by getting the balance wrong, and then the album would get lost.'

Hayley refers to the fact that it had been decided to market the album as a classical one in order to increase visibility. This involved some manoeuvring.

'We ended up debating a lot what the format should be,' says Dickon Stainer. 'We felt it needed to qualify for the classical charts because she'd go in at number one and we'd have a story. The rules are that sixty per cent of the repertoire has to be nominally classical – either a classical work or something with classical origins. We managed to argue that the Maori tracks were anonymous folk songs because Kiri Te Kanawa had released a record with those on.'

Such matters are administered by OCC, The Official UK Charts Company, who protect the definitions of musical genres, and whose decision would be crucial to *Pure*'s success. 'We changed the listing a few times,' says Stainer.

Pure is a very cunningly put-together album, touching an enormous number of bases, from the traditional Maori songs, which automatically appeal to New Zealand audiences but equally intrigue listeners in other countries, to its pop classic

'Wuthering Heights', to the classical adaptations from Ravel and Vivaldi, to the straight classical of Orff and contemporary composer Karl Jenkins. To achieve a coherence with such disparate material – as Martin and Class did – is a remarkable achievement.

'There's just so much variety, with lots of different sources and different people's ideas,' says Hayley. 'One of Giles's main jobs was making sure it sounded like an album.'

However, not all the credit can go to the masterminds behind the scenes. Hayley's voice, the reason for the recording, provides the energy that holds it all together. Initially Decca had hoped to reuse some of the Dublin work, but Hayley's voice was changing and there was a noticeable difference in the way she sang even after a gap of only some months. The vocals on *Pure* are all from 2003.

No one expected the album to have the impact on the UK pop charts that it did. Top 20 was the most anyone hoped for. When it reached number eight, it had already exceeded every expectation at many levels.

Hayley had been faced with difficult choices when selecting the material for the album that would perform this feat. 'It's hard when you've got a list of really good songs,' she says. 'Having to cut them down is tough. There are some gorgeous songs that were dropped so it could qualify as classical, but if I'd added another poppy song it would have tipped the balance.'

Giles Martin was also very aware that he had to present something that Decca would be happy with. One expensive wrong direction was enough. Recording began at Eastcote

Studios before moving to Sir George Martin's own Air Studios. Hayley could have been forgiven for being a little overwhelmed at Air, located in the London suburb of Hampstead.

'All of a sudden people would be coming in, cameras were filming and it was pretty grand,' she says. 'It's a converted church, so you're in a big room with stained-glass windows. You were kind of shocked to see the big orchestra and choir. That's when it really kicks in.'

'Up till that point,' says Jill, 'Hayley was working on a small scale. Now you realise it's a big scale. There's security at the door where you speak after pushing a button and a big iron gate slides open. And someone is at the desk watching everyone come in. There was even a separate café.'

'We got there,' says Hayley, 'and on the whiteboard it said, Studio one George Michael, studio two Hayley Westenra, studio three Cecilia Bartoli. And I met Bryn Terfel, who was recording there as well. That was the first time I met him, though I already knew I was going to be singing with him. I just thought, Wow, I'm here where it really happens!'

Day by day it was Giles and Hayley on the ground. Sarah Class made a few appearances at the studio during the orchestral recording sessions, but she is based in Bristol and for the most part would simply send her arrangements from there. Hayley and Giles would discuss them and occasionally suggest changes.

The biggest difference between recording at Air and Hayley's earlier experiences – and she had made three albums in three years, not counting the aborted *Pure* sessions – was the amount of time taken over each number. 'In New Zealand

I'd do three songs a day,' she says. 'In London it was a song a day, or sometimes we'd go back to a song the next day and try new things.' Despite the pressure behind the scenes, the mood in the studio was relaxed. 'I'd go through a song and if there was a bit I wasn't happy with I could re-record it,' says Hayley. 'And Giles would offer suggestions on how to sing a certain phrase.'

Only 'In Trutina' (from Orff's *Carmina Burana*) was sung live with the orchestra. For the other songs, Hayley sang with the orchestra then did a separate vocal take in case there were sections she wasn't happy with and wanted to change later. One unexpected difficulty arose with the number 'My Heart and I'. For some reason composer Ennio Morricone was reluctant to part with the music, even though rights to the song had been negotiated. 'We had to get someone to listen and write down the lyrics and arrangement,' says Hayley. 'I'd be singing and there was a word we thought was "aimlessly" but could have been "endlessly". We thought, Is it this or that? It was safer to record the vocals and music separately in case we needed to change a word. It was a bit of a palaver.'

A choir made up of London-resident Maori was another stroke that added richness to the texture of the album as a whole. Like Hayley, they were a touch overwhelmed. They could hear a professional choir singing in another studio and one choir member said, 'We haven't had all this training. We don't sing like that choir out there.' But Giles Martin told them, 'I don't want you to sing like that at all. What I want from you is emotion.' Which is what he got. To a UK audience, the Maori component of *Pure* lends it a slightly exotic flavour. 'No one had heard Maori songs much before,' says Hayley. 'They do find it quite mystical and haunting.'

Most stories about *Pure* mention Sir George Martin's involvement, often to the point of implying he was the producer. Hayley is the last person to want to overstate his contribution, but at the same time she is careful to acknowledge it.

'He wrote a song on the album ['Beat of your Heart', co-written with Giles] for a start, which was a huge honour. Then he arranged "Amazing Grace". And because we were working at his studios, he'd pop in to see how things were going. I didn't spend a lot of time with him, but when he was doing the "Amazing Grace" arrangement, he came and met me and had a few ideas and asked my opinion. And I was just, "Yes, that's great." I didn't really feel like I could change anything! And all his ideas were great and worked really well.'

There are several versions of *Pure* for different markets. There was no point, for instance, including 'Pokarekare Ana' and 'Amazing Grace' yet again for New Zealand. Also, the 60 per cent classical requirement was not necessary for Hayley's home country.

'And in Asia,' explains Hayley, 'they need as many bonus tracks as possible, so there's extra tracks from my other two albums. That's to make it different, because they've also got imports and the imported ones are cheaper than the local releases.'

While Hayley had a much greater involvement in the selection of songs for *Pure* than she had on previous albums, there is one compromise song. '"Never Say Goodbye" I didn't like at first, but everyone convinced me it was a good song. That was the compromise one. It grows on you.'

When choosing material, Hayley always looks for a musical challenge. 'Most of these songs have got something to think about, like "Benedictus", which has got this great dynamic. There's always something to work on.

'All the tracks on *Pure* were relatively challenging in different ways. "My Heart and I" needed a relaxed way of singing, whereas the classical songs you sing classically. Then there's "Who Painted the Moon Black?", which is poppy, and I'm not that experienced with that, even though I love pop. We included "Hine e Hine" and "Pokarekare Ana", because for a start "Pokarekare Ana" is a gorgeous song, and I wanted to include "Hine e Hine" because it was another Maori song. It's nice to have a Maori element and a bit of my heritage on the album.' Hayley has a Maori great-great-grandfather on her mother's side.

Overall, Hayley says, 'It was great having the whole mixture. I love the violin solo at the beginning of "Dark Waltz". It's a bit eerie. Then there's tracks like "Moon", which is a sad song but still quite light-hearted. Chris Neil discovered that. It was one of the very first ones that everyone liked. It's slightly poppy but still easy listening. We fiddled around with which key to put it in, to make it sound warmer.

'A lot of the time on tracks we'd add different instruments. On "Moon" they brought in a guitarist and suddenly it sounded like a completely different track. The guitar is a thread running through the album.

'It's nice having a pure classical song on it, like "In Trutina", as well as "Benedictus". I've met Karl Jenkins, and he's keen for me to record more of his work. He's a modern classical composer, and originally it was a choral piece. It had never been done as a solo piece before, so that was a bit exciting. It had four parts to make up this one mass of sound. It's mellow and still in some respects, then has this big impact halfway through the piece.

'"River of Dreams" is "Winter" from Vivaldi's *The Four Seasons*, with words added. It's a way of giving a classical element with a little twist. All these are things people haven't heard before. It's introducing the public to a new sound.'

As for the album's name, once someone said 'Pure', there was never any other possibility. The word was a perfect description of the material on the disc and the voice that sang it.

For Hayley, the recording of *Pure* was a happy experience because she had a lot more input than she had been allowed previously. She was getting older, and her suggestions were met with respect. Previously she had lacked the confidence to advance opinions different from other people's, especially if they were about a matter that was their area of expertise.

But, for all this apparent deference to the artist's wishes, there was one song on *Pure* that Hayley had to fight for single-handed. Just as 'Mary Did You Know?' was a pivotal choice on *My Gift to You*, *Pure* will be remembered by some for a far more heated dispute over a song.

Kate Bush's 'Wuthering Heights' was a favourite that Hayley had loved from the first time her mother played it for her. (She had also studied the book on which it is based at school.) When they were staying in Kensington, she and Jill would come home at night, put on a tape of the song and dance around the flat singing along to it. One night Hayley said, 'Oh it's midnight, the neighbours might hear,' and then just carried on, singing and dancing.

For anyone to attempt to cover a song so firmly identified with its original singer would seem audacious in the extreme, but Hayley wanted to do a version of it for *Pure*. The idea was too audacious, certainly, for the folks at Decca, from Costa Pilavachi down. They said no. Hayley said yes.

'In the end,' says Hayley, '"Wuthering Heights" was a big issue on the album. It was when we'd got everything recorded – only then can you present it to people who judge whether it's classical or pop. You can't take one song in at a time and say, "Is this classical?" So we were at the point where we had to take songs off. And "Wuthering Heights" was one that the UK team worried about because people would see it on the CD and go, "Oh, so that's the kind of album it is."'

'We all thought "Wuthering Heights" was a terrible idea,' says Dickon Stainer. In record companies, no one wants to be responsible for an expensive mistake. A seed of doubt can quickly grow into an oak of industry terror as executives scurry to play it safe. This, it seems, is what had happened with 'Wuthering Heights'.

Inevitably, a meeting was called at the London headquarters of Universal Classics and Jazz, of which Decca is a part.

'You have to picture all these suits sitting around a table in an office,' says Pilavachi, who attended along with Hayley, Gerald and Jill, Sophie and Isaac, plus Dickon Stainer and Bill Holland, who runs Universal Classics and Jazz. 'Our mission was to persuade Hayley not to include "Wuthering Heights". And even her parents were beginning to waver, listening to our logic about why it didn't fit. These were solid, conventional arguments.'

'I could see we were against all this lot,' Jill recalls. 'It was scary pushing something when they could be right. They market albums all the time, we don't.'

But, 'Hayley was adamant it should be on,' says Pilavachi. 'She stood up against everyone. It was very impressive to see her. She was overcome with emotion and stood her ground.'

When Hayley's eyes began to water, no one knew where to look. Someone passed the tissues. Then Costa tactfully said, 'We don't have to make this decision now. We can leave it till tomorrow.' That was the end of the discussion.

'I think I decided within .5 of a second [of the tears],' says Dickon Stainer, 'that it should be on the album. She felt very strongly, personally, and she was completely right, and we were completely wrong. And people love it. It was the strength of her feeling that convinced us.

'She's a strong, individual, heartfelt artist with strong ideas. I look back at that and think, There's someone who knew her own mind at sixteen. There's a sense of destiny about her.'

'In the end,' says Pilavachi, 'we said, "If you feel that strongly, who are we to say this? Put it on the album." I called her that night and said, "I've never felt more proud of you. You stood up to all of us, and you should always do that if you believe in something. It's your record at the end of the day – we're only the facilitators. We often talk about that. It was a watershed in our relations with her. We learned to listen to her more and trust her more. It was almost like a coming out.'

'The "Wuthering Heights" issue was before my time,' says Steve Abbott, 'but the record company calling her in, and all those suits lined up against a young girl, saying, "We don't want this track on the record," should never have happened. She knows what she wants and every decision she's made has been right – "Wuthering Heights" especially.'

'One of the reasons *Pure* took a long time,' says Pilavachi, 'was because Hayley was young and didn't really have very established ideas about who she wanted to be and what she wanted to do. She was more reactive than proactive.'

The battle for 'Wuthering Heights' marked the end of the reactive phase of Hayley's career.

CHAPTER NINE

The Machine Kicks In

Pure would first be released in New Zealand on 17 July 2003, with the UK release planned for September. Universal NZ mounted their biggest launch event ever, at the Auckland Art Gallery. Hayley sang accompanied by guitarist Kurt Shanks, whose day job was bass player for Boh Runga's band Stellar. Shanks had been sent a CD from which to learn the songs and met Hayley just twenty-four hours before the launch. He has since become a stalwart of the band for her Pacific and Asian performances.

'There were discussions about releasing it in the UK first, then here at Christmas,' says Universal marketing manager Alister Cain, who masterminded the release with his team. 'Then we realised we couldn't do the right promotion. Also, we felt we had a responsibility to lead the charge. So we pulled out all the stops and it was a great night. It set the tone that this was an international release.' The CD duly shot to number one.

'That said,' continues Holt, 'there were concerns around October and November that awareness had dropped and it had done its dash. So we released the bonus disc and that boosted it again.' The bonus disc included UK versions of 'Pokarekare Ana' and 'Amazing Grace', which had not been on the original New Zealand release, as well as 'The Mummers Dance', 'Mary Did You Know?' (a UK version), 'Silent Night' and 'Away in a Manger'. Record stores intimated that this dead horse should no longer be flogged, 'But we were staunch about it,' says Cain.

Universal's belief in their artist paid off all around and saw *Pure* carry on to set a New Zealand record of eleven times platinum sales within a year.

The record company had the advantage of world-class images and supporting material from the UK, where lavish amounts had been spent on styling, grooming and photography. They advertised aggressively on TV, as well as on radio and in print.

And once *Pure* started setting records internationally there was also a slew of free publicity in the form of news stories which Universal's publicity department made sure were always available to New Zealand's press-release-friendly daily newspapers.

One thing Universal did not have much of was radio support. Hayley's band of crossover was not a good fit with any of the niches in New Zealand's widely fragmented radio market. But one presenter, John Budge at Auckland-based Easy Listening i, took a fancy to 'Who Painted the Moon Black?', and gave it extensive air play on that station and Classic Hits, which helped move things along. 'I just thought it was perfect for us,' says Budge. 'Like so much new New Zealand music, there was a feeling of confidence that hasn't always been there.'

Hayley wasn't played much on influential student music station bFM, but she made an impact when she visited. 'She had an amazing effect on all these black-dressed, overgrown goths,' recalls presenter Damian Christie, who interviewed her. 'She was an absolute delight, and everyone was swooning around her. Everyone down to the grumpy programme director was sitting around grinning when she left. It was like they had all had a little dose of Prozac.'

Hayley played numerous showcases with Kurt Shanks to launch the album in New Zealand and Australia during July. Shanks's overriding impression of her was of the quality of her musicianship. He cites one sound check in a theatre empty of all but technicians and others preparing for the show, whose work came to a standstill as Hayley's voice filled the room. Launches themselves are notorious for being about the free food and drink to those who attend, to the point that the music can barely be heard over chewing and the clinking of glasses. Hayley never failed to get the room's attention.

'She was a dream for Universal to promote,' says Cain. 'She'll do anything, to the extent where she doesn't mind getting gunged on [children's programme] *What Now?*, or going on the *Breakfast* TV news show. She can mix in any circles.' (Hayley was used to being gunged on *What Now?* As a young child when she went along to watch filming for fun, she would be the kid picked out of the audience to be covered with slime, or 'gunged' – a phenomenon cited by the family as early evidence of her natural, attention-getting star power.)

Universal had high expectations of *Pure*, hoping for 60,000 sales by targeting the fans who had bought the first two albums. Expectations were quickly exceeded. 'In launch week we did 30,000,' says Adam Holt. 'We got to 60,000 by October or thereabouts, and by Christmas we had sold 145,000 copies. It was bigger than anyone expected. It was obviously the right market at the right time. But we were flabbergasted.' *Pure* would soon become the best-selling album ever by a New Zealand artist.

'If we just had the new album and not the overseas story,' says Cain, 'we may have just done the 60,000, but New Zealanders love an overseas success story.'

'It took a long time from the signing till the album came out,' says Alister Cain, 'but once the machine kicks into gear, it's unstoppable. Sometimes, you get a plan in place and a couple of things fall over and it doesn't happen. But with this one, when you get a great record, amazing talent and natural person, in synch with a push from a multinational company, it's pretty hard to stop it. When you say go, it goes.'

Pure was launched in the UK in September. Initially, it was a tough sell – who was going to buy a CD by an unknown New Zealand teenager with a musical style whose boundaries were not familiar to audiences? As in New Zealand, vital mainstream radio play would prove elusive. But having invested this much in the recording, Decca was not about to stint on promotion.

Steve Dinwoodie is a freelancer who was responsible for the

album's regional radio and TV promotions. 'The original sell into radio was hard,' says Dinwoodie. He admits resorting at first to an old wheeze. 'To get over the initial resistance, we asked people to look at whether this was the new Charlotte Church. But Hayley was very different, so we soon distanced her from that.

'The first thing radio stations get with a new release is a promotional pack that looks the same as all the other promotional packs and just goes into a pile. But a few years ago at EMI we had done some small three-inch CDs for Queen and Beatles releases. They were very collectable. So we did that for *Pure* and it enticed people to play it directly, because of how it looked.' That mini-disc now fetches healthy sums on eBay.

Midweek UK chart figures are released on a Tuesday. Dickon Stainer was mildly stunned to learn that the week it was launched *Pure* was at number 12, and not in the classical charts but in the pop charts.

'I said, "It can't be."' But it was, having sold 3000 copies on its first day. Stainer looked back through the figures and saw that the record for best-selling first week was held by . . . Charlotte Church.

'We met on Wednesday with Gerald and Hayley. We knew if we broke the record we'd have a story [to capitalise on for more publicity]. We also realised it would be touch and go, because we'd have to sell a lot more on Thursday, Friday and Saturday. We immediately booked more TV advertising, against all financial logic.'

Despite all the push that a record company publicity machine can give, it was Hayley's own initiative and energy that provided the final impetus to put *Pure* into the record-breaking position it still holds. (Dickon Stainer predicts that by the time its sales life is over, *Pure* will be not just the fastest-selling but also the best-selling UK classical release ever, with the exception of the unassailable Three Tenors.) Hayley took the same attitude to her major label début that she had taken to shopping-mall talent quests: If you want something, do everything you can to make it happen. She recognised how disappointing it would be to miss beating Charlotte Church's record by just a few copies and took matters into her own hands.

She asked Gerald to get her a list of major London record stores, and on Saturday, on her own, got on the tube and proceeded to make a circuit of stores. She would go in, introduce herself and offer to sign copies of *Pure*, aware of the traditional wisdom that a signed CD is a sold CD.

'The good thing about Hayley was that she was prepared to do anything,' says Stainer. 'Some artists aren't, and then they wonder why they haven't had any exposure. HMV stores would call and say, "We just had a young girl in from your company called Hayley."'

'How many artists would do that?' says Gerald.

Sunday was chart day, and the Westenras were having lunch with another freelance publicity person working on *Pure*, Lisa Davies. 'We were sitting having a drink in our garden on a lovely summer's day,' says Davies, 'and Costa phoned for Hayley and said, "Good news. You're number eight in the UK album chart." For a new artist to go straight in like that in their first week – no one really believed it. A Sting or Elton might do that. There was a moment of disbelief while it sank in.'

At 19,420 units sold, Hayley had beaten Charlotte Church's record by 300 copies – many of them, without a doubt, signed ones.

'We had a press release prepared to say she'd broken the record,' says Dickon Stainer. 'It went straight out over the wire. We also have a text-based TV news channel here that tends to beat the papers. By seven that Sunday night, just as the chart was being published officially, there was an item on Radio 1 saying an unknown New Zealand girl had broken the chart record. The next day, things went mad, there were people ringing up, spreads appearing in national papers.

'A lot of people in other companies would have looked at the results and thought, Who is this? In this market, a lot of big albums come out in September and people are setting them up at a very competitive time of year. For her to launch from nowhere meant that everyone in the business was going: Who is that?'

Despite the difficulties in getting initial exposure, one of Hayley's advantages was that when people heard her they were hooked. 'If you were to have a conversion rate from exposure to buying the album,' says Stainer, 'hers would be very high. They probably only needed to see or hear her once and that was it.'

No one was more delighted than Costa Pilavachi. 'On the day we got the first week's chart results, which were so far above expectations, I told Hayley, "Honestly, I really mean this, in my career I don't think anyone deserved the success as much."'

But one person whose expectations were not exceeded was Jill. She hadn't dared have any.

'I was just relieved,' says Jill. 'I probably exhaled. It's kind of disappointing that I didn't think about it more, but there was always something else we were working on. I did hope it would do well. And we didn't want to let the record company down. That was important to us.'

As the tube-tour story demonstrates, although Decca provided the vehicle for *Pure*'s launch, it was Hayley who had the energy and will to make it the phenomenon it would become. The next few months would be a gruelling period of promotional work that would daunt the hardiest, most ambitious performer. The Christchurch teenager seemed to take it all in her stride.

Promotional activity for *Pure* was in preparation even before the album was recorded. 'I started in 2002,' says Lisa Davies, 'because there was talk of the album being released that early. I started chipping away at TV. There were people who had seen her with Russell Watson, and I got a couple of major TVs on the strength of that.

'Then plans were made to go in 2003. She came over [to London] and that's when my work really began. We had some tools because of her success in New Zealand, such as footage of the concert with Russell. We did selective showcases, cherry-picking our special contacts. And everyone was really taken with her.'

This groundwork paid off in bookings for TV appearances which brought Hayley to the notice of the right people, including singing with another former child star, Aled Jones, who was reinventing himself as an adult performer. This led to a duet with him at the Classical Brit Awards (for which Hayley herself would be a finalist the following year). She also appeared on the popular religious programme *Songs of Praise* – which, as Davies notes, has as big an audience as *Top of the Pops*.

'Everything was set up perfectly,' says Davies. 'None of it was massive, but it was all to the right audience. And Hayley delivered every time – one thing would lead to three others. Soon we were getting all sorts of requests, from pop shows and young children's shows to the older end.'

Davies found Hayley's story easier to sell because of her background, not despite it. That her family was 'normal', rather than super-privileged, helped, as did the fact that she came from somewhere so far away. Ironically, Jill had once said to Hayley about coming from Christchurch: 'Of all the places to live when you want to have an international career . . . '

Steve Dinwoodie set up a tour of regional radio stations for Hayley. 'There are some forty local BBC radio stations,' he explains. 'We thought they would be the best possible route for her, and started getting her on to shows two months before *Pure* was released.'

One hurdle quickly overcome was media scepticism about the quality of Hayley's voice. Steve Dinwoodie knew many in the industry would suspect its unusual purity was the result of studio sleight-of-hand. 'Radio programmers know how records are made and the tools that can be used,' he says. 'But we showed them that Sir George Martin was involved, and part of the press pack was shots of her in the studio with the orchestra. They were won over quite easily.'

And any lingering doubts were dispelled by Hayley's party

piece. 'She made a big impression with her ability to sing a cappella,' says Dickon Stainer. Steve Dinwoodie was on the road with Hayley, and Stainer recounts a phone conversation with him during which Stainer could hear *Pure* playing in the background. 'I said, "Where are you? Are they playing the album?" And he said, "No, she's singing in the studio. This happens everywhere we go. She sings and the phones light up."'

'The reaction is always gauged on radio by people taking the time to ring in,' says Dinwoodie. 'And we could literally see the phone lines light up solidly every time.'

The phone calls were from people wanting to know who the girl with the amazing voice was, but also, promisingly, whether she had an album they could buy.

Hayley had already made a big impact in Wales, where love of the singing voice is an integral part of life. 'They have their strong rugby singing culture and that's permeated to the general culture,' notes Stainer. 'Bryn Terfel is without a doubt one of the most famous people in Wales. They are fanatical about him.'

Receiving Terfel's stamp of approval, therefore, is a big boost for an artist in Wales. The month before *Pure* was released, Hayley had been invited to sing with him – and another idol, José Carreras – at his annual music festival, Faenol, held over three nights and attended by some 15,000 people on each of them. That their Bryn was bringing this unknown girl to sing with him attracted huge interest in the Welsh media, putting Hayley on the front page of all the papers. If she was good enough for Bryn, she was good enough for them.

A few days prior to Faenol, Hayley had been touring Asia.

Hayley just after singing 'Amazing Grace' as a tribute to Sir Peter Blake at Coca Cola Christmas in the Park, Christchurch, 2001.

Hayley on stage at the end of the Christchurch concert of the
Hayley Westenra tour, 2001. She is joined by her siblings, Isaac and Sophie,
and Ben Morrison, Tim Beveridge and Shaun Dixon.

At the 2001 New Zealand Entertainment Awards where Hayley was awarded the Rising
Star of the Year Award. Also pictured are pop group Zed, who won Group of the Year.

Sky City Starlight Symphony, 2001. Hayley's first Auckland concert.

With top UK classical singer Russell Watson and former Steps member Faye Tozer, at Russell's concert in the Auckland Domain, 2002.

Hayley, a confident and assured performer, at the Russell Watson concert, Auckland Domain, 2002.

During the filming of a TV commercial to promote her album *Pure*, 2003.

With José Carreras and Bryn Terfel after the Bryn Terfel Festival concert, Wales 2003.

Hayley performing with José Carreras at his Royal Albert Hall concert, 2003.
After the concert José presented Hayley with her official platinum sales award
for sales of *Pure*.

A promotional shot for Hayley's *Pure* album. *Pure* was the best-selling classical album in the UK in 2003, selling more than one million copies. It has gone more than ten times platinum in New Zealand.

In the dressing room at the London Palladium during her *Pure* tour, 2004.

At Air Studios recording 'Beat of Your Heart'. Sir George Martin is conducting the song he co-wrote with his son Giles Martin, the producer of *Pure*.

'We worried how she'd hold up,' says Gerald, 'but she was fine. She was singing "Ave Maria" as a trio with Carreras and Bryn. We went to rehearsal the night before, and it was only then she found out she had to sing it in Latin instead of Italian, which she was used to. She was very nervous – because of who she was singing with and because of the new lyrics – but she got up and sang it beautifully. It's remarkable the way Hayley pulls it all together at the last minute.'

On the northern England regional radio circuit, Hayley continued to astound by throwing off a perfect 'Pokarekare Ana' every time she was asked. The hard work paid off, building a sizeable base of people eager to buy the album when it came out.

'A lot of those stations have one or two key shows,' says Steve Dinwoodie, 'and get people in and out in two minutes. Hayley was getting thirty minutes, sometimes more than an hour. She was entertaining, informative, and got to their target audience. Her interview style was always relaxed. She induced people to wonder how it had all happened.'

Back in London, Dickon Stainer was quietly excited, but until *Pure* was released no one could be sure whether this interest would be translated into record sales.

Lisa Davies believes one of the reasons Hayley went down so well on radio was that when she sang live, presenters, used to a parade of world-weary celebs with books and barrows to push, felt she had done something personal for them. It was her ever-present willingness to make a little bit of extra effort paying off again.

'The real class of an artist is when they feel at ease and can do that naturally,' says Dinwoodie, who has worked with the likes of David Bowie and Pink Floyd, and can recognise the will to succeed when he sees it.

Not long before setting off on that promotional round, Hayley had performed at the Classical Brits, singing a duet of 'Pokarekare Ana' with Aled Jones. It was a big night.

'Beforehand there was a red-carpet entrance,' says Hayley. 'It was the first time I'd done the red-carpet thing. We had a rehearsal, then had to come out and get into a limousine and pretend we were driving in. There was a Maori welcome organised and all these photographers lined up.'

Although she was not included in the TV broadcast, the audience on the night was full of industry heavyweights. She had been seen by a large number of international figures several months before *Pure*'s release. So, although many of the general public were yet to become aware of her, within the industry there was a great deal of expectation and anticipation. 'We knew she'd be big,' says Stainer, 'but no one else there knew.'

For Hayley the highlight of the night was getting to meet one of her all-time idols. And for once she can remember every word that was spoken.

'Andrea Bocelli was also performing, and I really wanted to meet him. Someone from the record company took me into his dressing room after I had performed. They introduced me and he said, "You have the voice of an angel." So there we go. End quote.'

Other appearances during this time ranged from the venerable children's programme *Blue Peter* – on which she sang

'Wuthering Heights' – to the *Parkinson* Christmas special, to an incongruous guest spot on *The Frank Skinner Show* alongside Justin Hawkins from The Darkness. Hayley particularly enjoyed her duet with the off-key – and notoriously not-pure – comedian Skinner.

'Her time was well spent,' says Jill. 'If you get opportunities, you've got to go for them, and these were big opportunities. Frank Skinner really enjoyed her. She has this pure image – which is a terrible image to live up to – and he expected a staid person, but she is nice. She won't be swearing or trying to be cool, but she has a sense of humour and understands different people are interviewing her and will respond differently for them.'

Hayley makes this all appear so effortless it's easy to overlook the hard work involved. Many teenagers can barely say hello to strangers, but she has spent years conversing comfortably and at length with them. Only occasionally does the strain show. And, characteristically, what annoys her when it does is not the personal inconvenience but the possibility that she is letting others down.

'I got sick the first week of my promotion in the UK,' says Hayley. 'It was so annoying because I'd be going on a TV show and I could hardly speak because I had this raging sore throat. And everyone would say, "Oh you sound fine," but I knew I could have done a better job if I'd been well. You just have to plough through and keep going.

'I kept on singing because TV shows are so important. Although I didn't want to make a bad impression by singing terribly. I had to record my four bonus tracks for *Pure* as well at the tail end of that sore throat. After that experience I decided I'm just going to have to stay well. It makes you really aware of how important your health is.'

One of the things that made Hayley's job with the UK media easier for her was simply that she has nothing to hide. 'I did wonder how I would cope,' she says. 'In New Zealand we get the impression the UK media are harsh, and the paparazzi and gossip mags are. It was a bit scary sometimes – journalists can come across nice, then write a really cynical article. But everyone was really nice and there wasn't a bad article written. People were probably trying to catch me out, but there's nothing to catch.'

She also coped well with being asked the same questions over and over again – about comparisons with Charlotte Church or how she got her start busking. 'Sometimes it's a little bit tedious, but I'd always try to think about the question with a fresh mind. You don't want to go into the auto mode of just answering a question the way you always do. It obviously worked.'

She received one kind of signal that she had 'arrived' when she was interviewed for a spread in celebrity bible *Hello* magazine. Its photographer's ingenuity was stretched trying to find enough angles for its obligatory several shots in the tiny Westenra flat.

'I thought, *Hello* mag, wow, that's where you see people like Victoria Beckham, and then there's me,' says Hayley.

Of her experience of the UK press in general, Hayley says, 'All the journalists were really nice, though some might have taken a bit of convincing. You cross your fingers that they'll write a nice article and aren't just being false.'

Coming up with a different story for every interview is one of the first rules media trainers will try to teach someone. Decca, in fact, decided the normally compulsory media training wouldn't be necessary in Hayley's case because they didn't want to tamper with the refreshing natural quality she brought to interviews. But Hayley has her own set of rules as well. She is careful to avoid saying anything that might be able to be twisted, having seen other artists have their words come back and bite them in print.

One anecdote crystallises Hayley's relationship with the UK media. A journalist renowned for writing negative articles was going to be interviewing her for a story that would get her a lot of coverage. It would be good publicity if it were positive. But it never went to print because he couldn't find anything negative. There was no dirt there.

CHAPTER TEN

The Natural

Hayley's international success in many ways is a repetition of that at home. The same qualities she brought to bear as the Littlest Star and a McDonald's Young Entertainer are still at work, polished and magnified for the world stage. Some of these can be taught, others can never be learned and must come from within. The dichotomy is perhaps best summed up by a family friend: 'She's a natural, but she also works at it.'

Foremost among the strengths that no one could have taught her is her ability to take control of a crowd with a minimum of fuss, whether at South City Mall, Christchurch, or the Royal Albert Hall, London.

'I remember her doing a charity thing for a hospice in 2001,' says Gray Bartlett. 'It was a difficult situation, with just a piano up on stage. Other performers had brought discs and had big sounds. But she just clicked perfectly. That crowd had had all this big noise, and then they get to this . . . She just knocked them for six.'

'She sang at my football ground, Celtic, in front of 60,000 people,' says Steve Abbott. 'They didn't think she could do it. A friend said, "We don't want to compromise your artist." Some people haven't pulled it off with that crowd. You've got all those people singing "You'll Never Walk Alone" out of tune and out of time. It was like *Apocalypse Now* with everything going on around her, but she rose above it, and they loved her.'

Hayley's confidence has developed over the years. Of early performing she says, 'If something didn't work, I wouldn't take my time doing my bow. I'd just scuttle offstage. Generally, I don't think too much about what I'm doing onstage, but things like talking to the audience are important. I've developed that. People like it and hopefully it adds something.'

Hayley doesn't milk an audience. Rather she brings them to her by acknowledging that performing is a form of communication, and thus has to work in two directions at once. 'I don't do the cheesy things: "Are you all having a good time?" That works for pop concerts, and sometimes it's good to get the audience involved, but I'm not overly outgoing on stage.'

Steve Brooker, business development manager of the Christchurch Symphony Orchestra, has seen Hayley working in all kinds of environments. She has made numerous appearances with her home-town orchestra, from children's concerts that introduce young people to musical instruments, to singing 'Away in a Manger' for a Christmas special, to Christmas in the Park. One year, her potential involvement in a Christchurch Symphony performance was questioned because there was concern she had been overexposed.

Brooker says in each environment there is one constant: 'She is always absolutely consistent in her performance. She never sounds as if she's underprepared or the environment doesn't suit her. That makes her a model artist if you're a promoter. She's always had that maturity beyond her years – not the false maturity some of these kids get.'

Those qualities Hayley was not born with have been quickly acquired. Richard Jay Alexander notes she is an excellent learner. 'She listens,' he says, with the palpable relief of a director who does not find this quality to be universal. 'A lot of people have their own ideas, which is great, but some people don't listen. She learns on her feet. If she'd been singing a song one way and I had suggestions and said, "I think you'll get more money out of that note if you attack it like this," the adjustment was immediate, not gradual. She knows her tool. That was extraordinary to me.

'I remember saying to her when she sang "Pokarekare Ana" with Russell Watson, "Whatever you do, Hayley, he's a powerhouse, and on that last note do not back off because he'll eat you alive. Not in a mean way but he'll blow you off the stage. And in the footage of the special – you can see she almost gets knocked off her feet extending the note.'

Composer Ronan Hardiman noted a mature level of interpretation in Hayley's approach to the lyrics of her songs. 'When I get a new song, I want to make sure I totally under-stand it,' says Hayley. 'People can have different interpretations, and I like to have mine and get that across. With quite a few of the songs on *Pure*, when I first got them I was like, "What's this all about?" Then you come up with your own interpretation. There's no point doing what everyone else has done.'

All this adds up to a high level of enjoyment in her work. To see Hayley Westenra onstage is to recognise somebody who's doing what they would rather be doing more than anything else in the world.

'A lot of people kick into performance persona,' says Richard Jay Alexander. 'But with Hayley it's an extension of who she is. You can't beat honesty and truth, and it seems to emanate from her.'

'You want to sing the music you enjoy,' she says, 'rather than what people think you should enjoy. You have to listen to your public, but at the same time sing stuff you're excited about, not just earn as much money as you can as soon as you can.'

If she has a favourite kind of performance it is the large out-door concerts like Christchurch's Christmas in the Park, where her appearances have become a highlight over the past few years. 'Even when it's dark, you see the glow sticks waving, and if it's early you can see the whole audience, and the children running around. It's a party. Everyone's there to have a good time. Sometimes it's a little tense – when you walk out onstage and people clap, then they all go silent and that's the big moment. But you don't worry about them being super-critical, because they're just there for some entertainment and enjoyment.'

There's only one thing that matters to Hayley after a performance: has she done as well as she could? 'I'm happy as long as I know I've done my best. It's awful if you think you could have done better. There's relief, too, because it's all built up to that, including the days beforehand.'

She's not a diva personality and she doesn't make a diva's demands. Her concert rider is not extensive. 'There's basic things like bottles of water, and some fruit is nice. Sometimes they'll want to include a meal, so we'll get vegetarian sushi or rocket salad, which I like, or sandwiches, though wheat's not good before you sing because it can bloat you.

'Then there's the technical rider, like what kind of microphone I use. That's pretty much it. Oh, and a full-length mirror and good lighting – basic things.'

A mirror and lights might seem like they could be taken for granted, but in Hayley's experience, they can't. 'In Wellington once, we ended up in this tent with no electricity. It was really windy, and I had curls, so I wanted to touch up my hair with curling tongs. I had to hairspray it and hope it would stay. I was a complete mess. That's when we learned to put electricity on the rider.'

Nerves are seldom a problem. 'The first note or the first phrase – that's the hardest, because as long as you've sung that well, it builds up your confidence.'

One exception is when Hayley is singing to an audience she needs to impress, whether it's record company representatives or people from Disney considering her for film work. 'Each concert seems to be really important,' she says. Before she went to the US in 2004 she was apprehensive about singing the US national anthem for Fox TV bookers. 'Everyone would be relying on me to make this big impression,' she says. 'There's all these showcases where there'll be someone I need to impress. They come backstage and say, "We're really looking forward to hearing you sing." It's this big build-up. That's the hardest part.

'You just have to get past it. As long as I've practised and am confident with what I'm doing, it takes away some of those nerves. I thought it would get easier, but each occasion seems more important than the one before.'

As she faced her US launch, Hayley finally had something she had long needed: a manager. Steve Abbott had joined the team around the time of *Pure*'s release. Jill and Gerald had performed the impossible in navigating her this far through the murky waters of the international music industry.

'In a weird way, their naïvety and lack of experience worked for them,' says Richard Jay Alexander. 'The mum and dad are a unified unit, and the kids are very much part of it. They've figured out how to make it work. It just seems to be a rock-solid family.' But the family unit could only do so much. It had been obvious for some time that despite Jill and Gerald's ability to shepherd Hayley so far a more experienced hand was needed to guide her through the challenges that lay ahead.

A couple of early candidates for the position hadn't worked out for various reasons which usually came down to personality differences. Anyone who took on Hayley would have to be able to work with the family unit, and respect how much they would continue to be part of her career. Gerald had given up his jewellery retailing business to help with Hayley Inc. 'I was juggling too many balls and it wasn't being fair to my partner, Jacek,' says Gerald. 'It was a big relief when I dropped out. Sure, I had built the business up and it was disappointing to have to let it go, but kids come first. A business is just a business, but kids are for life.'

'One of the difficulties getting top management,' says Adam Holt, 'was that the parents' involvement meant the deal wasn't that good. We told Jill and Gerald they'd never get a good management deal on that basis, but they did.' It should not have been a surprise – they had already been doing the impossible for several years.

The right person turned out to be Abbott, who had the perfect balance of music industry experience and family orientation. He also saw Hayley as a person first and a client second. Abbott's career had included playing with punk band UK Decay at seventeen, having his own label (which had a worldwide hit with the EMF song, 'Unbelievable') and working with artists as diverse as Pavement, Jeff Buckley and classical composer John Taverner. He still manages Heather Nova, an artist Hayley admires, but was at a career crossroads in 2003 and looking for someone new to manage.

'There's something about management,' says Abbott. 'The thrill of following someone from the beginning to the top.'

That someone needed to be a performer whom he could throw himself into managing with the 100 per cent involvement that is his trademark. 'I went out and got offered the obvious artists of my generation looking to reinvent their careers, but nothing grabbed me. At Decca they suggested a few people and I said, "What else have you got?"' He was played Hayley's 'Pokarekare Ana' and became intrigued. He discussed her over lunch with Costa Pilavachi, and on the strength of that the head of Decca recommended him to the Westenras.

But Colonel Tom Parker he is not. 'I was going to come to New Zealand a couple of weeks later because a friend lives here, but didn't want to put myself in their face. I'm no good at selling myself, and I know they're very sensitive to the hard sell. So I decided not to come down.'

Eventually they met in London, where Hayley played him the video for 'Who Painted the Moon Black?'. It was an awkward introduction because Abbott could see faults in the video. He was honest about it, but the conversation never got off generalities.

While he was trying to woo the Westenras, friends in the industry were trying to wean him off the idea because they believed co-managing would mean he would make less money than someone with his experience could expect. This didn't bother Abbott. He is happy to have a deal that acknowledges that much of the hard work has already been done, and he doesn't have to establish his artist from the ground up. As it has turned out, despite the misgivings of others, the deal has been completely satisfactory.

Universal UK boss John Kennedy had been Abbott's lawyer in a previous incarnation. He tried to talk him out of managing Hayley, but Abbott stood firm. 'At the end of the meeting, he said, "Okay, if you really want to do it, I'm going to send an e-mail to Adam Holt in New Zealand and send one to Costa and say, I'll vouch for this guy, he can do the job and I think you'll get on with him."' The only person left for Abbott to convince was Hayley.

About a week later, Gerald rang suggesting another meeting. 'Tomorrow's good,' said Abbott. In fact, five minutes would have been good. He called on father and daughter in Covent Garden the next day. Gerald asked a lot of questions about breaking Hayley in America, a market Abbott knew well. Hayley had some pertinent queries too.

'I've lived with the music and it's all about the music,' Abbott told them. 'I don't know either of you, but from what I hear about you I think I understand what you want. I understand I'll have to work for the family.'

Hayley finally interrupted, saying, 'I just want you to be my manager.' Gerald well-ummed that they would need to talk to Jill and do a few other things first, but Abbott left the meeting so excited he walked into several wrong doors before he found the lift. (Abbott has a knack for inadvertent slapstick. One early meeting took place at a function where champagne glasses were stacked on a table. He had an umbrella in his raincoat pocket and managed to send glasses flying as he made his way in to impress his prospective client.)

One day after their last meeting, with still no decision made, Abbott knew Hayley was due to appear at a Universal sales conference. He was having a bath when he decided to give Gerald a ring, just in case. He offered to come to the conference, where he could introduce Hayley to several important people he knew would be there.

'Come on down,' said Gerald, 'we're leaving in twenty minutes.'

'So I quickly got dressed. I remember running to the subway still wet. At the conference we were waiting for Hayley to do her bit. I said, "What shall I introduce myself as?" and Gerald said, "Well, the manager." It was almost like it was lucky I turned up that day and got the job, otherwise I might never have heard about it.'

From that point, says Abbott, 'It was twenty-two hours a day Hayley. The way I work is, I don't just send artists out on their own. If they're touring, I want to be with them all the time, because as stuff comes up they need a compromiser. It's especially important with female artists, because people always think there's someone pulling their strings. And with Hayley being sixteen, it was trebly so.

'I was keen to get there and understand what she wanted. She does hold her cards very close until you get to know her. Now I can look at her and have a good idea what she's thinking.'

Hayley has been thrilled with the choice, and not just for herself. 'I don't know how we would have coped without him,' she says. 'Dad and Mum are still heavily involved but you need someone with experience in the music world. The workload is huge. I don't know how Mum and Dad could have looked after us and done all that. Before, we were relying on Decca to make the right decisions. It's reassuring to have Steve, who knows what he's doing and can say we should be doing this, or shouldn't be doing that.

'Because he's got a bit of experience, he will say we shouldn't release in America at this time because sales are down [across the board]. It would have been difficult for Mum and Dad to say that, because they don't know.'

While dealing with short-term issues day to day, Abbott is also putting in place a long-term plan that will see Hayley through the years ahead. That means, for instance, turning down many lucrative sponsorships she has been offered because they don't fit. 'She is sixteen,' says Abbott. 'She is pure, and everything we do has to be into that. I think she will get rich – she works harder than anyone I've ever worked with – but it'll be a year or more.'

He believes her family has given Hayley attitudes that make her immune to many of the normal star traps. 'A lot of these prodigy families can be a nightmare. But there's a genuineness with the Westenras. The majority of parents are divorced and have money as the god. Hayley doesn't have any respect for money. Try to buy her something when you're out and it's a nightmare. Her outlook about doing things is based on the value of doing it rather than on doing it for the money.'

Just as Jill and Gerald were parents who acted as managers, Abbott is a manager who sometimes takes on a parent's role. 'Because diet is so important for her voice, I always make sure she eats well. She'll work all day, and unless someone says, "You need to eat," she'll just stay hungry. She'll take a sandwich reluctantly, and it'll be gone in a second. She inhales food.

'When I got involved, there were all these stylists and make-up artists around, and the first thing I wanted to do was get rid of them, because whenever I saw her in the mornings when she walked out that was Hayley. When you try to get someone else to do it, it doesn't work.

'She has a natural sense of so many things that she can do whatever she wants to do. I've got to make sure she's outgoing about what she wants to do and try to keep away people who'd try to mould her.'

Hayley's ability to deal with nerves is legendary. It's often observed that she remains calm while chaos goes on around her – and she does seem to attract a high level of chaos, especially when travelling. She has a knack for cutting things fine, and at least once has arrived at a venue only in time to have her dress zipped up for her as she walks onstage.

Once, when she was going from Dublin to Paris for a performance, the person responsible for loading her luggage had neglected to stow her dresses in the cab that was taking her and the family to the airport. The cab driver rang back to her hotel and asked for the dresses to be put in a taxi.

Everyone except Gerald, who stayed behind to collect the garments when they arrived, was checked through, and there was still no sign of the taxi. The plane was due to leave in fifteen minutes, but the cab was still half an hour away. Then a quarter hour's delay of the flight was announced. When the taxi did arrive, Gerald collected the frocks and raced to a counter where he was told firmly to get to the back of the queue. Eventually he got on to the plane just as the doors were closing – to the relief of the other passengers, who were by now all aware of the drama.

Whenever Hayley travels she is likely to be away for a long time, so the family always has the maximum allowable amount of luggage. Jill spreads everyone's clothes evenly through the bags, so that if one goes missing everybody will still have something to wear. There is always at least one costume for Hayley in hand luggage.

Hayley is not a star who reclines in the sanctuary of a VIP lounge while others do all the work. On tour to promote *Pure*, Steve Dinwoodie recalls her as a hands-on diva. 'We were due to fly from Heathrow to Scotland and the airports were fogbound at both ends. We were trying to change our flights, and

Hayley got so involved in everything she took over talking to the guys behind the desk: "Can we get on this flight? Can we get that one?" Flying back that evening, they were again delayed a few hours, but she was totally unfazed. Some American artists would be suing everybody in sight in a case like that.'

While the weather is out of her control, Hayley might reasonably expect that events she attends will be well organised. In fact, they are often anything but. Charity events, which are run on a shoestring everywhere in the world, can especially strain an artist's goodwill.

For one such event, Hayley was sent the song she was to perform well in advance. But the rather doleful tune with its morbid lyrics just wasn't her, and, even at the risk of offending the organisers, she told them she wouldn't be able to sing it. She didn't get her substitute until just before she was due on-stage to rehearse with the orchestra.

'She got through the rehearsal,' says Lisa Davies, 'and learned the song properly between then and the performance. Then they asked her to sing another song. They told her she'd know it because it was a really famous hymn, but she'd never seen it in her life.'

It was at that performance that Hayley met Vera Lynn, then eighty-six, who was very impressed by the young singer. 'Of course, Hayley didn't know who she was,' says Steve Abbott. 'But Vera Lynn's seen them all, and she said of all the singers she's seen, who've stepped into that world, Hayley's the first one she's felt really pulled it off.'

In late October 2003 Hayley did a week-long promotional

tour of Japan, where, by a bizarre chain of events, she was a household voice, if not name, to viewers of the drama series *Shiroi Kyotu* (The White Tower).

'My version of "Amazing Grace" is the theme for the series, which is set in a hospital,' says Hayley. 'Twenty per cent of the population watch it, which must be fifteen to twenty million people. When I went to Japan for a week, I went to meet the cast. I watched the series and it's so funny, because they play the song at the end with the credits, but they also sometimes have it halfway through as part of the episode. There was a scene where this guy came home from work and they played the whole thing.'

Just how popular the programme and its theme are became apparent when Hayley was doing a magazine shoot in Japan and the photographer, who had not been taking particular notice of her, began to shake uncontrollably when he found out she was the singer of *that* song. 'He got incredibly emotional,' says Gerald. 'He got down on his hands and knees and was bowing as low as he could.'

'It took him five minutes to recover,' says Hayley. 'It's incredible having that effect on someone.'

Hayley went to Tokyo and Osaka and loved every minute of it. 'Everyone's so polite and there's the whole bowing thing. The whole experience was great – the food, people, and how they like giving gifts.'

'She loved Japanese dishes,' observes publicist Hiroko Kawachi, who accompanied Hayley in Japan, 'especially tofu. And, she ate mozuku – a kind of seaweed, a bit sour but very healthy – on a morning TV show. The host of the programme and other cast were surprised to see Hayley liked it. It's a very Japanese food.'

As she does everywhere else, Hayley had been working on her local phrases. Hearts melted when she finished her mozuku, put down her chopsticks and said, 'This is yummy,' in Japanese.

Hayley's connection with *Shiroi Kyotu* brought automatic media interest. That she came from New Zealand rather than the UK or US also piqued curiosity. She did music shows, breakfast TV, radio and print interviews, and put in an appearance at a Universal conference along with Sting and Busted. As elsewhere, according to Kawachi, she made a great impression 'because she was so natural and answered every question very sincerely. She was very friendly, so everyone became fond of her.' This attitude, adds Kawachi, goes a long way to winning the affection of the Japanese audience.

Hayley was marketed in Japan with the line 'Pure voice – only one in the world'.

'In Japanese, this phrase has a nice ring,' says Kawachi. 'And she has proven it true.'

Hayley also visited Taiwan on this trip, and her schedule there was as packed as the streets. 'There were full-on things every fifteen minutes,' says Hayley. 'In New Zealand there'd be half an hour for an interview. This was bang, bang, bang. One person would be finishing as another was arriving. I enjoy the Asian countries because they have a translator, so I don't have to talk as much. Talking is tiring on your voice, and sometimes I'd have to sing in the evening for a showcase as well, which is tough if you've been talking the whole day.'

But Hayley takes it all in her stride. 'Hayley definitely keeps it together,' agrees Steve Abbott. 'When you're on the road she's the one you can always rely on to get things done. Gerald and I do our best, but we're in our forties, we forget things. Jill has fifteen things going on at once. Hayley has the focus. The chaos won't get any better, because the world's going to get crazier around her.'

Hayley's ability to withstand chaos was greatly tested in the promotional round for *Pure*. But Jill's was tested even more. 'When I arrived in London once to take over from Gerald, I had to go through Hayley's cases, and most of her clothes needed washing. Hayley thought she was doing us a favour by not putting all her washing out at once. She said she didn't want to shock us. I said, "No, keep it out so there's no nasty surprises like this."'

There was chaos of a different sort when José Carreras, no less, changed a song he was to sing with Hayley the night before they performed together in December 2003.

'The concert was arranged quite a while back, but a lot of it was organised at the last minute,' says Hayley. 'I was told I had to sing "Tonight" from *West Side Story*. I was panicking because it's a big piece and I didn't know how I could learn it in time. Then I got to rehearsal and José Carreras was all, "Oh, you want to sing 'Tonight', do you?" And I'm like, "What!"

'We performed "Ave Maria" together and "Little Drummer Boy" – that was a new one, but I knew the words. Then "Silent Night" got thrown at me.

'In the end I sang "All I Ask of You" at the last minute to replace "Tonight". I think someone suggested it and I said, "I know that." So the next night we were performing it after one rehearsal, hoping I'd remember the words. And I had to perform "Oh Holy Night". I came in at the wrong place and had to pull myself together and keep going. The conductor put his hand up and I thought he meant "go" but he meant "wait".

'I always go offstage thinking I could have done so much better – I could have held that note for longer, or that word didn't come out well. Small things annoy me. But that's life.'

Adding to the confusion, Decca wanted to take the opportunity to have Carreras present Hayley with her platinum disc for *Pure*. 'The big concerts are the ones where you need all your concentration,' says Hayley, 'but the big concerts are also the ones that attract the record company and all those important people you have to meet at half-time. I was straight on for the second half. It would have been nice to get a bit more time to think things through, but they wanted to get a photo of José Carreras and me with the double platinum disc. We'll learn next time. It was hard because we were leaving straight after as well – or the record company people were. It was a big deal.'

'It was all happening at interval, when she should have been changing,' says Jill. 'Then suddenly the stage manager was there, saying, "We want her on," and Hayley's going, "What am I singing?" She hadn't had time to get her head around it. And her singing teacher, Mary Hammond, was also there for the first time, because she thought she could be helpful. That almost made it worse, because she wanted to get Hayley into another room to go over something. And Steve's thinking she needs to be on her own for a few minutes. It was too much. Steve said, "This won't happen again."'

For Hayley the evening did not end with her final bow. Outside there were fans with 'Hayley Westenra International' in gold on their jerseys, who'd driven four hours to get a video to put on their website and to give Hayley a present. Hayley had been delayed backstage and the driver said, 'If you'd come ten minutes ago, there'd have been a hundred more.'

If such mini-fiascos were followed by periods of calm it would be one thing, but Hayley is often bounced from one round of hectic activity to another like a pinball, as Jill's description of events in the days following the Carreras concert demonstrates.

'The next day she had to do a photo shoot for *Classic FM* magazine, but before that she was looking at some music for a song she was going to be recording in three hours and listening to it on Steve's laptop. She said, "They don't match, so which one do I follow?" That was the song she was going to record for *Mulan 2*, the new Disney film. She should have had a week to prepare it.

'We had to get to the studio and to a fitting. We were meant to have a quick meeting about the dresses but missed it because they were in another room and we didn't hear the buzzer – luckily, because we didn't have time for it anyway. And when we got to the studio, this guy was saying, "Try and make it a little bit smoother," and I said, "She normally does sing beautifully and smoothly but she's just got the song." By the end of that session it was late and her voice was knackered.

'Then Steve got a call and we had to rush off to do two Christmas carols for Australia by satellite. We got home about midnight and Steve got a call from the studio: "Can she come back in now?" He said no.'

Hayley was due to return to New Zealand soon and every day counted. She declined an offer of a first-class flight home if she would stay another day to do more recording. Naturally, she was keen to get back to familiar surroundings, but she also knew she had to honour a commitment in Invercargill and was worried about missing a connection if she altered her booking. Sophie and Isaac were among the headline acts at a Christmas concert, and Hayley was determined to be there to support them.

CHAPTER ELEVEN

A Lot to Learn

With such strains, it's a wonder Hayley has any voice left at all. Fortunately, her early vocal tuition has been supplemented by coaching in London with teacher Mary Hammond. For singers, learning about their voice is something that never stops.

'When I'm recording,' says Hayley, 'I prefer to have someone to guide me. Giles recommended Mary. She's lovely and I go to her every couple of weeks or when I get a new song or feel I need advice. The good thing about her is that she's got experience in lots of styles – she's studied opera but also teaches Coldplay's lead singer, Chris Martin, and does a lot of work in musical theatre. But I often rely on my instincts and what feels comfortable. My voice seems to know what to do.'

Hammond was instrumental in one of the few near-misses of Hayley's career – she won and lost a part in the *Phantom of the Opera* movie. 'Mary Hammond was talking about the movie and said they were still auditioning. I was, "Oh wow!" She gave me the number of the guy doing the casting and I phoned him, but they'd decided on a Christine [the female lead]. We sent an audition pack, and they called me back saying they were having trouble with the negotiations with Christine. They asked me if I would be interested, but then they settled and offered me the part of Meg, a ballet dancer, instead. I spent two weeks doing ballet every day to get this little part. They offered me the role and sent me the script, but then the record company was concerned that there would be clashes with promotions for *Pure*. Filming was in September, so it would have been a complete clash. It was disappointing at the time, but if I'd done it, the album wouldn't have been the success it has.'

Dame Malvina Major's groundwork, as she predicted it would, was starting to pay off in 2003. 'I've had help to learn how to breathe. When I first went to Mary she said, "Oh, you're already doing that right." She gives me advice about scientific things like voice placement – the voice should feel like it's going out the back of your forehead. And you have to raise your cheekbones to raise the soft palate. All these little tips are useful, but generally I just sing.'

Hayley says it's important to keep tension out of the voice, a trap into which it's easy to fall. 'Occasionally there've been notes I've struggled with in a particular song. Sometimes there's a particular word, and you want it to sound like the word so people know what you're singing about, but you have to adjust it to fit your voice. I've got a long way to go in terms of making sure I'm always supporting my voice. Even opera singers like Bryn have teachers they go to. Even when you've got a great voice there're things to work on.'

During the London months, Hayley's heavy schedule of performing – up to an hour and a half a day – meant there was no need for further practice. But when she's at home in Christchurch she sings around the house to 'groom my voice and keep a check on it. When I've done it, I feel good, quite fulfilled. I'm working on it and getting there. It's one step closer to being where I want to be.'

Practices follow a set routine. 'A lot of the time I just do half an hour of exercises working on certain notes, voice placement and warming up. Then I might go over some of the songs from my album. You have to, because you might go to a performance and wish you had done some practice – you do forget things if you don't keep it up.'

A good example of the sort of challenges that require practice was 'The Star Spangled Banner', which Hayley had to learn to sing for the Fox TV network in the US in early 2004.

'It's quite challenging,' Hayley says. 'It depends what key I sing it in, but the word "glare" is an awkward vowel for the note. I thought, I could just change the key, but I didn't know if I could or not.'

And even the family can have enough. 'One night Mum was on the phone and Sophie was trying to get to sleep, having an early night, and they forced me to stop. It was 9.30 and "The Star Spangled Banner" didn't help.'

Although Hayley's voice is absolutely true, she never takes it for granted. 'Sometimes I feel edgy about certain points in a song. And because my voice is still developing, there are some songs I found easy when young that I now have to work on a little bit harder. Sometimes, if it's a new piece, and there's a certain word on a certain note and your voice doesn't know what to do, it might drop and go a bit funny. That makes you nervous – you hear about people who lose their voice in performance or open their mouth and nothing comes out.'

Because Hayley has been recording and recorded since she was so young, it is easy to trace the development of her voice. Martine Carter notes that from the age of about twelve it developed great strength. 'To hear her sing in a small room is deafening – you can't believe the power she has.'

At fourteen Hayley could comfortably reach high E. 'At the moment my voice isn't changing drastically,' she says. 'It's just developing and getting maturity, getting a little bit richer, a little bit deeper maybe. It's at a point where it's settled, but I've developed a poppy style as well as the classical and I can chop and change. Before when I sang pop, it had a more classical edge. Now I try to make the pop sound poppy.'

A strong instrument can still be a delicate one, none more so than the human voice. Hayley goes to great lengths to safeguard her general health, and protect her voice in particular. She has inherited Jill's interest in research when it comes to health matters, from awareness of potentially dangerous chemicals in sunscreen – which she applies assiduously – to the qualities of herbal teas.

She keeps to a vegetarian diet, though not fanatically. 'I'm a pesco-vegetarian, because I still eat fish for the oils and some protein. And I eat eggs. I don't drink coffee or straight milk. I avoid dairy, but if there's a little bit of chocolate with dairy in it, I'm not that strict. I have a real weakness for chocolate.'

Jill has always sought out herbal remedies and tried to keep the family to a healthy diet, which has had obvious benefits for Hayley. 'If she was, like, "Let's have pizza tonight," then we'd have pizza,' says Hayley. 'But because she's talked so much about how important a healthy diet is, we've become interested.'

For her voice, Hayley has a catalogue of nostrums. 'Apple cider vinegar is good to cleanse your throat and for general well-being; liquorice tea; slippery elm's a good coating for a sore throat. You can burn lavender oil and tea-tree oil and have a steam inhalation.'

Malvina Major advised fresh pineapple for a sore throat, supplementing Jill's recommendations of ginger tea or echinacea. 'When you're tired, the voice is the first thing to go,' says Major.

And Hayley is not a good sleeper, helped in part by the complexity of her schedule and the fact she is often working until late at night.

'Even if we get back at 11.30 – if it's Mum and I, we'll always discuss things and have something to eat. It does take a while to wind down, because you've been on this high. Somehow I just have to get into a routine of going straight to bed, but I take ages to get to sleep. I went to bed last night at 9.45, which is early for me, but I wasn't asleep till 11.30. Plus if you're staying in a hotel room, which is nearly every night for me now, it's so tempting to turn on the TV, and I become hooked in to whatever is on and have to watch it to the end.

'Flying is another big health aspect. It's really easy to catch something from recycled air. I've got a mini-air purifier which I can wear around my neck now – I'm going to do whatever it takes to stay well. You have to be well beforehand and have an immune system that can fight things. I can't get sick, so it's really important, and when I'm home I get back into exercise.'

Hayley was back in Christchurch for Christmas 2003, trying to slow down after her tumultuous year. But after just one day at home she was off to Invercargill to hear Sophie and Isaac sing. Then she had two days at home before heading off to Timaru, where Christmas day would be spent with Jill's mother.

Plans to catch up on schoolwork, answer mail and even tidy her room were disrupted by planning for her New Zealand tour and the need simply to put her feet up, take advantage of Alan Traill's offer to use his swimming pool or have a game of tennis with Isaac.

Hayley has been trying to look after her formal education. In recent years she has been able to manage only sporadic attendance at Burnside High School.

'I went for the first day and met my teachers in 2003,' she says. 'Then I said, "Actually I'm off for four months." It was weird because I wanted to get settled in, but knew I was about to leave so if they were saying something was due at a particular time I knew I'd be away so I didn't need to do it. I came back during the year and did three weeks, but it's hard to be focused and motivated. It was good having some time with my friends more than anything.'

Hayley appreciates that when she is at school in Christchurch her teachers treat her as just another one of the kids – which is exactly how she feels. The most they might permit themselves is a dry, 'We haven't seen you for a while,' but for the most part they just let her be part of the school.

Her parents would like her to complete her formal qualifications but the reality is there hasn't been time. Manager Steve Abbott is sympathetic to the aim but feels 'exams are something we're all doing [with Hayley] because we feel we need to because of her age'. He has pointed out that she will always be able to do exams, but will not get a second chance like this one for a career.

A tutor, Matthew Slater, was engaged in London, but with only limited success. 'We'd schedule in lessons of two or three hours at a time,' says Hayley. 'But it's really difficult fitting it in. If a TV show comes up, you don't want to turn it down. At this time, it's more important than schoolwork – we prioritise.'

Under her own steam, Hayley managed to catch up on enough work to pass her NCEA level one exams. 'I don't know how, but I managed to pull through French, maths, English, science, music and German, even though I skipped a whole year. I think I just learned what I had to learn for the specific exam. I enjoy French and German because I feel I can apply them to what I'm doing.'

She still has a bit to learn. 'When I went to Paris I practised my French and I mucked up,' she recalls. A lamp in her hotel room didn't work, so she rang reception and said in her best French that it was broken as in 'shattered', not broken as in 'not working', and a staff member arrived at her door with a vacuum cleaner.

Ironically, the subject it has been most difficult for Hayley to do well in under NCEA has been music. With its constant internal assessments, it requires students to be present on certain days. 'You can't change a major concert overseas because you've got NCEA as a member of the choir,' says Jill. And no credits are given for musical achievements outside school.

A couple of years ago, Hayley was at school on the day everyone was given a careers questionnaire. 'You answer a whole lot of questions, and they give you a list of things you'd be good for, in order. My top one was conducting, then musical director. Another one was map-maker. But they didn't have singer or dancer in the options.'

Not that it mattered. Hayley had been planning for a long time to go straight into a full-time music career when she finished school. When or if she finishes school becomes more and more uncertain as the career successes mount up.

Hayley has managed to fit in a little experience of the UK school system. Around the time of *Pure*'s release, she stayed with promotions person Lisa Davies and her two daughters. 'Dad had gone back and Mum was coming over. Lisa said, "You ought to go to school with the girls, but you probably don't want to." I said, "Yeah, it'd be cool." And it was cool to be back in the world of homework and revision. I enjoyed it because I wasn't the one having to do all the homework. I just joined in what I wanted to. But it reminded me that it's nice having a social life, and that's part of school.'

Lisa's daughter Charlotte, in whose class Hayley spent time, was also pleased with her decision. Charlotte is no fan of German but Hayley was happy to sit next to her and quietly help her out with answers in class. Hayley would have liked to spend longer at school but promotional duties called. She sums up her attitude to missing out on formal schooling in a not unexpected fashion: 'It's hard fitting back in, because you're away and it's all exciting, and you come back and it's . . . maths.'

It's hard being a school kid and a celebrity. There are good and bad bits about the latter. Good bits include things like upgrades on planes and in hotels – though Hayley is often left feeling guilty because she will be moved up to the suite with the fruit and aromatherapy packs while Jill or Gerald will be left in the small standard room.

The bad bits include being held up at airport security checks while starstruck staff – 'Do you know who that was? Hayley Westenra!' – take longer than usual to check through her bags so they can be in 'the presence' a little longer. Not that they would ever admit to acting so unprofessionally.

Hayley is used to it now, but a vivid early memory of being recognised in Christchurch came when she was in a bakery trying to buy some bread, 'and this person looked at me. Then they went behind the counter and I heard them whispering. It was like a chain reaction. People kept coming out from the back of the shop and staring.'

Styling and grooming requirements come with success, but, as Steve Abbott has noted, are best left to Hayley. Occasionally, however, she has no choice but to hand herself over to the professionals. 'Like with the shots for *Pure*,' she recalls. 'They had make-up artists and stylists. Sometimes magazines bring in their own people. Sometimes they say, "You're fine the way you are," and you end up looking completely washed out. Or they go to the other extreme, with thick eyeliner. Stylists can be useful, though. Like there're these dresses I wear that the stylist got at sample prices. My wardrobe's grown a bit in the past year.'

Hayley loves her butterfly dresses by UK designer Jenny Packham. 'She's up and coming but at the same time has a bit of a profile,' says Hayley. 'She's doing well but still keen for me to wear her clothes, which is very nice. They're gorgeous dresses because they're not too old for me. My fave is one with butter-flies, sequins and beads. If I'm on TV, I might wear jeans and a top, but I also enjoy getting dressed up in my gowns. Finding time to go in and try them on is hard.

'When I'm in New Zealand, I can go into Annah Stretton stores and choose garments as Annah also supplies me with clothes – she supplied all my gowns for the Pure tour.'

She could get spoilt, but Hayley can still get excited by the little things. Like going to Packham's fashion show and getting a 'little bag with heated eyelash curler and nail polish and nail buffer and hair thing – it was, "Wow, this is so cool." It's fun when you get a few perks.'

Hayley has had devoted fans since *Walking in the Air*, which after all was a fan's idea. She has long since passed the point where she can reply personally to fan mail, and this is some-thing she regrets. 'I get quite a range of people sending letters and things. There're older people, then there're younger ones in their twenties, and then there're young girls who relate to me.

'People send framed pictures of themselves. When I was going back to New Zealand I could hardly fit my own stuff in my bag, let alone what people had sent me. My room's a decent size but there's no way you could fit all this stuff in.'

Fans' enthusiasm is demonstrated in many ways. 'It's weird when people come up to you and start crying on your shoulder,' says Hayley. 'You just pat them on the back. It's a massive compliment, so you can't complain. But it's weird to think your music has that effect on people, especially getting emails and letters from people who say it got them through their illness. One person said it lowered their blood pressure.'

There are several websites devoted to her, the first (www.hayleywestenrafans.com) established early in 2001 by Lindsay Gilliland, a New Zealand Charlotte Church fan who discovered Hayley by chance one day while surfing the Internet. He didn't hear her voice until her first *60 Minutes* appearance. Taken by her personality, and sensing something special there, he was prompted to set up the site. He rang the family, in the days when they were still listed, and asked their permission to set up the site. Hayley's reaction was typically aghast, 'For me?' she exclaimed, unable to understand why anyone would want to do such a thing.

The Westenras have never met Gilliland but appreciate the work he does and have supported the site with their characteristic dedication, even ringing the webmaster now and then with updates. Hayley contributes to the message board when she has time.

Gilliland has never seen Hayley perform, though 'I heard her singing down the end of the phone once when I was talking to Gerald.'

'We try to track every performance that's televised and get

bits from that,' says Gilliland. 'Various other fans have come on board. They've collected information and material and sent it to me.' The site is nothing if not comprehensive.

Despite all this interest, one of Hayley's most disarming qualities is that she has apparently failed to recognise the magnitude of her achievement. Each new success comes as a wonderful surprise, not as the fulfilment of an expectation. 'She can do something amazing one day and forget to tell you about it the next,' says Lisa Davies. Months after *Pure* was a hit she could still get a buzz out of walking into an HMV store in London and seeing a display of the album.

'Every day there's a new milestone with Hayley,' says Adam Holt. 'I said to Jill once, "Do you realise how amazing this is?" She said, "Yeah . . . well, not really."'

'It just seems a bit unbelievable,' says Hayley. 'It's all happened so quickly. When you're performing and in the midst of it all, you take everything in your stride and are quite focused. But when you step back and look at it, that's when it kicks in. It's pretty cool. From releasing my first album to singing with people like Bryn Terfel and José Carreras in a couple of years – it is a bit surreal.'

This apparent lack of awareness doesn't surprise Malvina Major. 'She never had huge expectations,' says Major. 'She was always, in a way, naïve about her ability. Talented people often don't realise their ability, so it's a shock when something fantastic happens. She has a wonderful innocence.'

Steve Abbott explains away Hayley's seeming insouciance by pointing to this special kind of naïvety. '*Pure* was fast-moving but she had nothing to gauge it by. The record sales sound like a lot by Kiwi standards, but she doesn't understand that people don't sell those kinds of numbers. And she hasn't spent ten years waiting for it to happen, so she can't make that comparison.'

CHAPTER TWELVE

Family, Friends and the Future

Still in her mid-teens, there is only one way Hayley could have coped with the pressures her success has put her under, and that is with the support of her family and friends.

'That support system is the most important thing,' says Steve Abbott. 'She can have every other asset, but if that's not there the whole thing will fall apart.'

It's easy for an artist of any age to lose touch with reality when they are surrounded by people who are eager to do things for them and ready to agree – at least on the surface – with whatever they say. There's nothing like a mother complaining about your not putting your laundry out to keep your feet on the ground.

And despite the lengthy separations, the family is still close. All three Westenra children have become accustomed to spending several months at a time with only one parent, and for Jill and Gerald themselves the strain is even greater.

'I think Jill and Gerald are like swans, who appear on the surface with everything cool but are paddling away like mad underneath,' says Dickon Stainer. 'They've made it seem straightforward, but it can't have been. I don't think when they get home they're discussing the charts. I think they're discussing whether the toast's burnt.'

Fortunately, everyone in Hayley's ambit, from Costa Pilavachi down, acknowledges the importance of the family and works to keep them together. Suggestions that Hayley could be sent overseas with a chaperone have been quickly rejected. As Gerald says, 'It's not like going off to boarding school.'

And while Steve Abbott and Hayley get on extremely well, says Gerald, 'It's not quite the same as having family with her. She comes across as being very mature, but I've seen her when she's not. She has insecurities like every other teenager. And Decca realise that for all this to work properly the family has to be involved. They've got the message quite clearly that we're around.'

If there is one part of normal teenage life that Hayley is missing out on, it is probably the company of friends her own age. Whenever she returns to New Zealand, renewing contact with them is high on her list of priorities.

'It's good all getting back together and just hanging out at each other's houses on the weekend,' she says. 'Nothing has changed. It's not like I've missed out on a huge chunk of life and its hard to slot back in. It's easy.'

Most of Hayley's circle have been her friends since she was very young, and nearly all share an interest in music and performing. They are probably in the best position to judge how much her success has changed her.

'After gaps it's as though she's never been away,' says Katie Lock, who can claim the distinction of having been onstage with Hayley in *The Littlest Star*. 'She's not any different, so it's not hard to pick things up again. She doesn't go on about what she's been doing, but she'll tell us if we ask.'

'In the last few years she's just blossomed,' says classmate Georgie Olsen, who met Hayley when the two were performing with Canterbury Opera together. Their friendship was cemented when Burnside High School put them both in its specialist music programme. 'She's always been the same down-to-earth Hayley. Her attitude and loyalty to all of us have never changed. When you talk to her, it's still talking to Hayley, even though she's world famous.'

British tabloid journalists might be interested to know that Olsen has a first-hand account of the naughtiest thing Hayley is ever known to have done. 'We went to the movies once, to *The Green Mile*. We were fourteen and really wanted to go, but it was R16, so we tried to make ourselves look older by putting on make-up. But when we got there, there was no way anyone would believe Hayley was sixteen because she was so small.'

There's a small minority of young people, most of whom don't know Hayley, who have a negative attitude to her which they are all too ready to express. Their assumptions are among the few things that make Hayley bristle.

'It's just typical of what people think of all people who've been on TV,' she says with commendable restraint. 'They think

I'm stuck up. When my friends at school play sport at another school, kids immediately go, "Oh, you're from Burnside. Do you know Hayley Westenra? Is she really stuck up?" It's the immediate thing they say. My friends have to stick up for me. I don't think I'm stuck up. But it's just a minor thing.

'"She's rich." That's the other thing. People don't understand all the costs involved. You read in magazines about celebrities with Gucci bags, but they've probably just been given them because they've done an ad. Some stars have heaps of money, but others just rely on things they've been given and advances. People just assume they must be loaded.'

Just as her parents' friends are left to fight off the accusation that Jill and Gerald are pushy stage parents, so Hayley's real friends are quick to leap to her defence when she's unjustly maligned.

'That gets to me because she's one of the nicest people I'll ever know,' says Olsen. 'I get very annoyed about other people saying bad things about her.'

Emma Carter notes that this attitude has diminished in recent times. And in general Hayley's friends get to enjoy her company rather than fight her battles. 'We go to each other's birthday parties and things like that,' says Katie Lock. 'We have sleepovers or go bowling or play mini-golf. But it has been quite strange watching all this happen to a friend. It's hard to believe in a way. Over the years she's constantly got a little bit more famous. And now she's away a lot and meeting the Queen. It's like a different life that we're not part of, so you can't understand it completely. But it is exciting.'

If you're a musically inclined teenager, Hayley is a good

friend to have. Olsen is a promising songwriter, and Hayley has put her in touch with several people who are helping her on the way. But everyone who knows Hayley has noticed that she's naturally considerate, whether it's offering to carry a publicist's luggage or to clean up after a picnic with friends.

'She was always very sensitive to others' predicaments, and able to accept people and their differences,' says school principal Trevor Beaton. 'That's not always the case with kids who are recognised for their talent.'

Lucy Carter, younger sister of Hayley's friend Emma, has proof of this. She was once competing in a music festival where she encountered some girls who refused to believe she knew Hayley. Hayley provided a handwritten note wishing her luck, which put the doubts to rest.

In fact, Hayley seems to find time for everyone. Fiona Mitchell would often see her in productions at the Christchurch Town Hall when she worked there as an usher. 'She would always come up to me and say "Gidday" and smile,' she says. 'When children these days acknowledge an adult they know, it's really something.'

For another family friend, Hayley's concern for Sophie and Isaac stands out. 'She's very supportive of her brother and sister. At her age, often you don't see that, because kids are learning about themselves and trying to be adults.'

Somehow she has retained her sense of fun through it all. Mild practical jokes are a specialty, whether it's pretending to be sick and alarming a London publicist with a full day of appointments, when in reality she's just outside their office, or having water fights with friends. As producer Jim Hall notes, she hasn't succumbed to the jaded attitude that can afflict even young performers after a short time in the industry.

Hayley's time in the industry can safely be predicted to be a long one. At the beginning of 2004, she could look back with satisfaction at the records *Pure* had set. It was not just the fastest-selling UK classical recording ever, it was the best-selling classical disc of the year and had gone double platinum. It was nominated for Album of the Year in the 2004 Classical Brits (an award taken by Bryn Terfel). The only recording by a New Zealander to have sold more copies internationally is Crowded House's *Greatest Hits*. *Pure* went ten times platinum in New Zealand in February, making Hayley the fastest-selling local artist ever. It also holds the record for most weeks at number one by a New Zealand artist. Only Shania Twain and Dire Straits have spent longer in the top position. *Pure* has also gone platinum in Australia and Japan.

But there was little time for looking back. America was the goal for Hayley in 2004. Following *Pure*'s success in other territories, this lucrative market was the natural next step, and towards the end of 2003 she was much occupied with preparations for repeating her UK success. A fulsome *New York Times* story in 2003 had led the way.

The US market is not just bigger than others, it raises different sorts of concerns – like teeth. It was a relief for Hayley to know that her teeth were deemed acceptable for the American market.

Then there was her size. She has a figure many girls her age would kill for, but knowing the American obsession with weight, it was only natural that Hayley would wonder how they would find her. She was to be screen-tested, which meant she would be judged not just on her singing but also on her build and whether or not she had 'the right look'. There wasn't a lot she could do about it – there were no burgers or chips in her diet to cut out.

And there was the New Zealand accent, which can be hard for Americans to understand. As it was, most people commented on her charming 'lilt' and 'twang' when she spoke.

Finally, there were the sharks to consider. 'The American record industry is full of artifice,' says Steve Abbott. 'It's hard for her, because when she shakes someone's hand and speaks to them, she means it. That's not always the case over there.' But as they had done elsewhere, Hayley's naturalness and easy charm won over hardened industry figures.

January was spent auditioning players for the new-year New Zealand and Australian tour. Once that was done, Hayley headed to Los Angeles where she did several showcases for, among others, Disney, Fox and Warners. She sang either with a ghetto-blaster backing or an acoustic guitarist. After four days of performing for music and casting directors, Hayley was offered two movies and a TV show. A booking was firmed up for the *Good Morning America* show. She couldn't have asked for a better start.

But then she really astonished the Americans. Accepting some of the offers – the producers of *Princess Diaries 2* had offered to write in a part for her – would have meant reneging on other commitments on her New Zealand tour, and there was no way the girl who had said no to Victoria Beckham was going to do that.

In New York she sang for industry representatives in the *Good Morning America* studio on Times Square. It was winter, and the change in temperature had got to everyone, including Hayley, who had developed a sore throat. A blizzard prevented several important people arriving, but the snow, seen through the giant window in front of which she was singing, provided a magical backdrop for Hayley's performance. Howard Shore, Oscar-winning composer of the music for *The Lord of the Rings*, was there, and so was Costa Pilavachi, keeping an eye on his charge.

Because the non-attendees had included crucial buyers from large chains Borders and Wal-Mart, Hayley squeezed in a trip to their Detroit headquarters before heading back to New Zealand to begin her national tour in February. The concerts, accompanied by Hinewehi Mohi, tenor Brandon Pou, and Sophie and Isaac were a sell-out success right through the country. This was a new, far more polished Hayley, her performances now honed from months in front of tough international audiences. At the same time, she was still the serene, almost unassuming performer she had always been, letting her remarkable voice do the work.

One of the Auckland concerts was attended by fellow New Zealand-born, UK chart success Daniel Bedingfield. For a time the pair were the subject of strong rumours that they were an item. They were not. The two had met in London, and Bedingfield and Hayley as a couple would have been a match made in pop industry heaven. That was enough for the gossips to draw the illogical conclusion. Those who knew Hayley tried to work out when she might have found room in her schedule to become an item with anyone.

'There was nothing to it at all,' says Hayley, who is astonished at the amount of interest the rumours generated. 'When a magazine article about it came out, I did ring him – to say that the story wasn't coming from me.'

As for the prospect of boyfriends in general, Hayley says: 'I really don't have time for anything like that. I wish I did.'

The New Zealand dates were followed by more in Australia, Japan and the UK during March. But, before she left, Hayley had one important duty to perform – she received a special award from Prime Minister Helen Clark to commemorate *Pure*'s ten times platinum sales.

Then it was on to the States for the serious work. Hayley notched up a remarkable number of achievements throughout the year. She had two further important showcases in New York at the inauspiciously named but hyper-trendy Joe's Pub, which is renowned as an intimate venue for acts on the way up (plus quite a few established ones).

In April she celebrated her seventeenth birthday by sleeping in, exercising at the gym and going out for dinner – all normal activities which her schedule often doesn't leave her time for. Birthday celebrations tend to be hit-and-miss affairs these days. The year before, she simply ran out of time for a family celebration. 'It's not that I'm past it,' says Hayley. 'I like my birthday. It's very exciting, but after a while it's not worth stressing about.'

Pure went into The Billboard Top 200 at a respectable 70 but, more importantly, into the crossover chart at number two. Its performance in the US has been more than satisfactory, although it has followed a path of its own.

'It's a little bit different from the UK, where you have to make it in the first week to be successful,' says Hayley. 'In the US it's a more gradual thing. You can't just do one TV show and leave it at that. Each time I do something, the sales skyrocket. When I did *Good Morning America* it got to 70 in The Billboard charts. When I did something on National Public Radio it went to number one on Amazon. I did something on CBS one Sunday morning and it went to number one on Amazon again. And my CD *Hayley Westenra* was at number 14 on import. It was a bit frustrating at the beginning.'

One highlight was the Radio Disney series of concerts in schools, when Hayley played eight cities in three weeks. She loved the enthusiasm of American audiences, in contrast to the relatively subdued UK and New Zealand crowds she was used to.

In June she received the 2004 Favorite Up-and-Coming Artist Award from the American Society of Young Musicians, an accolade previously taken by, among others, Pink and Josh Groban. It is made every year to an artist 'whose unique contribution to music, either vocally or instrumentally, has brought new inspiration to the music community, which other up-and-coming artists aspire to follow'. The youngest ever UNICEF ambassador, she performed at a memorial for another UNICEF ambassador, the late Peter Ustinov, and appeared with José Carreras at the Chicago Opera House. She was booked to appear with the Boston Pops orchestra later in the year.

In July she had to brush up her Elvish – 'not the easiest

language to learn' – for an appearance as vocalist in a series of concerts of music from *The Lord of the Rings*, under the baton of its composer Howard Shore, who has the same agent as Hayley. Shore had lunched with her after her New York showcase and attended her Joe's Pub début. She had committed to dates in Canada and the US, but had offers to do more *Lord of the Rings* concerts as far ahead as nine months.

In the same month Hayley headlined a free concert in her new temporary home, New York, in support of that city's bid for the 2012 Olympics. And she was due to be heard on the soundtracks of two disparate movies: Disney's *Mulan 2* and Shakespeare's *The Merchant of Venice*.

But the biggest event on her horizon mid-year would take place back in New Zealand, where she was filming a concert for the US Public Broadcasting Service's *Great Performances* series.

'Hopefully the PBS special will give *Pure* the push it really needs,' says Hayley. 'It's being broadcast at the beginning of December and it has a massive viewership. Most of the music will be from *Pure*, but we're also having a bit of fun and making it quite dynamic. The shows are big orchestral shows and we'll do some different arrangements, like for "Beat of Your Heart" we might have ethnic drums at the beginning as opposed to ordinary drums. Some songs will be just with piano, and others with an orchestra and choir. There'll be a big range, and I'll have a lot of input into the staging and music.'

On a later trip she was also to fulfil a lifelong dream of appearing with Andrea Bocelli, whom she supported at a concert in Christchurch.

While Hayley is happy to continue this level of activity, she has other ends in sight. 'I'll give it a few more years and then it might slow down,' she says. 'This year [2004] has been taken up with America, then my next album will be coming out. I'll probably have to do more TV shows and . . . maybe it'll be five years before it'll slow down, and I'll be able to say, "No, I don't want to do every show," and we'll keep it to a concert a week. It would be nice to be able to pick and choose a little bit.'

She was due to begin recording that next album, again with Giles Martin, in London in February 2005.

'I don't want to wander off too far from what I've been doing,' says Hayley. She has had a mountain of material from which to choose, 'but the key is to find songs that I connect with. One thing I do want to happen is to have a lot more input into the material and hopefully write some lyrics or music for a song. When I'm trying to get to sleep I come up with all these ideas for lyrics and turn the light on and scribble them down.'

Writing her owns songs is also important to Hayley because, owing to the way the finances of the music industry are structured, composers earn a large slice of the money generated by a hit album. She has always written songs – her first was about some of her toys, when she was about six years old. She writes the music first and the lyrics later, generally about her own experiences and feelings. Finding time to do it has proved troublesome.

'It's difficult when you're away,' she says. 'I bought a tiny keyboard off eBay because I was so desperate. It's got little drumbeats and everything, but it's not the same as having a piano to play. When I'm at home it's great, because I've got a piano. You sit down and you're playing around and really want to write something, but I know I should be doing my maths homework or something else. I don't have that much time for it, but it's my way of relaxing. I'm trying to learn guitar because it's so portable while travelling. Then it will be easier to write.'

But it's not just about the money. 'Writing your own music is more satisfying, more fulfilling. I'd prefer to be singing my own music than to have to interpret a song. Rather than expect other people to do songs that represent you, it's more sensible to write them yourself. If it comes straight from you and is completely you, it adds another dimension.'

The new album will be made with the same care and deliberation that went into *Pure*. 'I don't want to rush one out. The next album is a big deal. Everyone's going, "Is it going to flop?" or whatever. So I don't want to throw a collection of songs together just for the sake of it.'

Whatever order things happen in, the future is bright. When people ask her what she is aiming for, Hayley says, 'Just to go as far as I can go, and see. I don't know how far I can go. I'm going to take it step by step.'

CHAPTER THIRTEEN

Ten Dos and a Don't for Parents

When Hayley goes to the supermarket, she's likely to be stopped by people wanting to tell her how much they love her singing. When Jill goes to the supermarket, she's likely to be stopped by people wanting her to tell them how to make their talented children into stars. She can't do that, because she never intended for her child to become a star. She did however, want Hayley – as she wants Sophie and Isaac – to make the most of whatever talents and interests they have. If she has learned more than a few lessons along the way, it is not because she is a starmaker but because she was trying to be a good mum. With that in mind, a few of the things Jill has done to support her children – nearly all of them learned on the job – are given below.

1. Do anything

It doesn't matter what field a child is interested in. What is important is that they have something they love doing. Jill has let all her children try as many things as possible while young. This is the direct opposite of the advice a well-meaning person once gave her when Hayley was a child – that Hayley would never do well at any one thing because she was doing too many different things.

When Isaac – who has a beautiful voice but less interest in singing than his sisters – developed an interest in archery, his parents arranged for him to have lessons. 'It's important to let them try all those activities,' says Jill. 'They have the time when they're young. As they get older, school takes more time, and at tertiary level it's harder to be spreading themselves thinly because things become more serious.'

It's easy to forget that as well as various musical activities Hayley was involved in lots of sports when she was younger. It wouldn't have mattered to her parents if she had become a gymnast or karate champion rather than a singer.

2. Do everything

Once your child has found something that interests them, do everything you can to help them get the most out of it. 'If you're going to do it, do it well,' says Jill. 'Don't just put them onstage and expect it to happen.'

In Hayley's case, that meant Jill searched out every avenue she could to develop her daughter's singing experience. 'If they like the idea of being onstage, for instance, it's up to the mother or father to approach a parent of one of the children who's doing that and find out how to get involved. And look out for audition notices, drama schools, singing lessons, talent quests – all of that helps.

'If a child really wants to pursue a career in the performing arts, they need to be well rounded in terms of skills. It might be an acting role with a little bit of singing. If they're good at acting but not at singing, they might only need a few pointers for singing, but if they don't have them, someone else will have the edge. There's always that little bit of competition involved if there's only one role and a lot of people wanting it. If you have more experience, because you've been in a few shows and have had a few lessons to improve your skills, you'll have a better chance.'

Their mother's help made Jill's children more confident, and excited, about performing, and so it became a shared family interest, not something in which one child was favoured over the others. 'It might just have been that we found a song and Hayley would say, "Oh, I get out of breath if I dance in that bit there," and Sophie would reply, "I could probably do all the dancing for you." Everyone was contributing ideas.'

3. Do trust the child

Children will naturally discover what they're good at. All parents can and should do is give them the opportunity to find out by looking for clubs or taking them to classes – be they for painting or piano playing. 'If you let them try a lot of things, there'll be ones they don't like,' says Jill. 'Ballet might appeal for a while because of the dresses but then it gets boring to them. At that point, if they're good at dance, you might say, "Would you prefer jazz?" But if they're no good at all and not enjoying it, you just say, "Well that's fine. Try something else now."'

Children don't take any pleasure in pursuing activities they have no talent for, and parents can ruin their desire to try out anything at all by insisting they do this or that activity if they are not enjoying it. 'So follow their lead, and talk to them lots,' says Jill. 'Just to be involved in what your child is interested in is important. Let them make the suggestion, and if there's something they'd like to do, that's what you do.'

4. Do go with the flow

Don't try to put a child off an activity because you think it might not lead to anything in the future. One day, Jill thought it would be nice to make a CD of Hayley's twelve-year-old voice. She didn't do it so she would have a demo to show record companies. She did it because she thought it would be fun. She didn't worry about how much it would cost, or whether the family could deal with the practicalities – she dealt with those matters one at a time as they arose.

'If you think about whether it makes sense, you won't find the time ever,' says Jill. 'Just dive in and do what you can, as you can, and realise it will be a lot of work.'

5. Do have low expectations

When Jill was helping Sophie make her own CD in the summer of 2003, she kept reminding her younger daughter not to have any expectations from it, as nothing might come of it. There was no long-term goal. No one was expecting Hayley's demo to lead to anything either. Jill's aim back then was no more than to make it as good as it could be at each step. Likewise, she wanted Sophie to do something that was fun and would have a result of which she could be proud.

'In talking about what we did, I don't think people should think, "Okay, that's what we'll do, and our child will get to this level," because I don't think you should even aim for a level. You shouldn't think, "I'm going to make my child famous." What we did isn't necessarily a blueprint; it's just what we wanted to do.'

Jill also acknowledges that all this was easier because she didn't have a career to occupy her attention. She just wanted to enjoy time with her children. She was also mindful that once they had grown up it would be too late to help them.

'What you're doing has benefits aside from what you hope it might lead to. We didn't say to Hayley, "We're going to create a career for you," but the fact we're doing this for Sophie has boosted her confidence enormously. You're saying, "You're that special. We believe in you that much." Confidence is the most wonderful thing to have.'

Realistic expectations also protect a child from becoming discouraged if they don't become the next Hayley Westenra. 'Warn them,' says Jill. 'Don't set them up for too many failures.'

6. Do be there

Talented children are not clockwork success stories in the making, who will follow a path to stardom if their parents wind up the key and sit back. Talent is not enough, and there are lots of opportunities for damage on the way. So parents need to be fully involved if they are serious, whether it's taking their children to lessons and waiting outside during a class, or finding opportunities for them to perform before an audience. And they also need to think through what is going to happen along the way.

'Take the talent quests,' says Jill. 'Parents need to use their adult understanding to look at a situation and think: who are the judges? what are they looking for? We've done this a lot and have been wary sometimes of putting the kids in talent quests because of the judges. If the judges don't have the right sort of musical appreciation, and a talented person gets rejected, that could stop them going any further. You've got to remind them that perhaps they're being judged on things that are not what they think they're being judged on. They might be incredibly musical, but the judges might be looking at movement or how they relate to the audience.'

7. Do ask for help

When Hayley started performing, the person she naturally turned to for help was her mother. And her mother knew nothing about it.

'A lot of parents don't know where to start,' says Jill, 'and I didn't know either, but somehow I found out. We're not experts – it just evolved.'

Jill discovered that if you asked people for help they would give it. When she needed to know something she didn't just look in the Yellow Pages – though she did that too. She asked everyone she knew who might have the information she needed, and sooner or later, one of them would. 'There's lots of people who can help, if you start looking. You may get the wrong person first, but sooner or later you'll get the right one.'

In the process she learned not only about the music business but something important about herself – that she was capable of doing a lot more than she thought she was.

8. Do support yourself too

Jill and Gerald are so involved in their children's performing and other interests because they find it fun. There was no risk they would become resentful because they felt they were missing out on something by putting time and effort into their children. A middle-aged Hayley will never be reminded of what her mother sacrificed to get her where she is, because as far as her mother is concerned there was no sacrifice.

'There was a creative side to it,' says Jill. 'I liked being involved behind the scenes in shows or helping them choose what to wear, so it was an outlet for me as well. And my children liked having that help.'

If Jill has a concern about how single-mindedly she has supported the children, it is that she hasn't provided an example for them of how to combine being a mother with having a career – something she sees as a possibility for Hayley and the others.

'She hasn't seen me juggle like that. There can be advantages in cases where parents have a career and children, and I haven't done that. So I don't think I've done everything perfectly.'

9. Do prioritise

Any parent knows you can't do it all. A parent like Jill knows it better than most. Some of the normal domestic niceties in the Westenra home have had to give way. A neatly manicured garden, clear benchtops, tidy bedrooms for the children – the amount of time that goes into other activities doesn't leave much over for these things.

'You have to prioritise,' says Jill. 'The garden will keep. I'd love to have things perfectly tidy, but I can't physically do it all. As parents we've had to change our standards and learn to turn a blind eye. But now and then it gets on top of me.'

10. Do enjoy yourself

Jill's last piece of advice is not really a rule. It's something that should be self-evident – but, she notes with regret, many people don't follow it. The most important thing is for children and their parents to enjoy themselves. 'If they're really enjoying what they're doing as a child, there's nothing lost, because they're creating wonderful memories and having a full child-hood. I always felt my kids had a rich childhood because they had a normal Kiwi upbringing. You've got to enjoy the journey.'

And . . . Don't get a manager

Although Hayley needed a full-time, professional manager for a long time before she got one, Jill says it's a common mistake for ambitious parents to think a manager is the most important thing. Jill and Gerald learned a lot by fostering Hayley's career in the early days. Without their involvement, she would have missed out on all the benefits that came from having her interests taken care of by the people who care most about her in the world. Managers in New Zealand can't provide that sort of support because the market is simply too small for them to make a living out of any one performer.

Index

Index

Index

Index

Joy Tonks

As a brilliant young singer soprano Malvina Major won some of the most prestigious international competitions, and after outstanding début performances a stellar career was predicted. Then, on the brink of major success, she returned home to New Zealand with her husband Winston.

So began the Malvina Major 'mystery'. For fifteen years she worked as a farmer's wife and mother of three children, fitting in singing practice between twice-daily milking. She often practised in the cowshed and continued to perform locally. In her early forties she began a second international singing career and encountered tragedy on the way.

In this book Dame Malvina talks openly about her life, her dreams, the disappointments and the tremendous spirit that has kept her singing for almost sixty years. She relates fascinating aspects of the performing life, and behind-the-scenes stories reveal her humanity and humour.

ONE DAY AT A TIME

SUZANNE PRENTICE

Suzanne Prentice has been in the public eye since her early teens when she dazzled the New Zealand entertainment world with the hit single 'Funny Face'. Regarded with great affection by her fans here and overseas, it is hard to imagine that this multi-platinum, award-winning performer had become an overweight yo-yo dieter and had lost her confidence.

After working with Michael Barrymore, mentally and physically exhausted, Suzanne made a decision that would transform her life; she finally took control of her eating and health. Although she struggled to even walk around the block without resting, Suzanne took up the motto *one day at a time*, swallowed her pride and joined a gym. Within a year she was performing in body sculpting competitions.

This is a story for every woman who struggles with her weight.

KEEPING IT OFF

SUZANNE PRENTICE

The sequel to the best-selling *One Day at a Time*.

Suzanne Prentice was once living testimony to the fact that diets don't work. A frumpy 87kg, Suzanne could barely walk to the letter box. But three years ago the multi-award-winning singer went down to 45kg in weight by devising and following her own weight-loss plan. Staying on track isn't easy, but Suzanne understands what it is like to diet, lose weight and then fall into the downward spiral of losing and regaining hard-lost kilos.

Keeping it Off will help everybody maintain their desired body shape and enjoy a healthy lifestyle. Understand the issues behind overeating and craving the wrong kinds of food – discover tactics for staying on track. Experience the joy of being fit and energetic.

Charlotte's Secrets

Charlotte Dawson

An honest look at some of the issues confronting young women today. Charlotte Dawson, all-round media goddess, has led a life crammed with glamorous highs and terrible lows, all lived through the pages of the popular press; intensely private details of her marriage break-up filled Australian papers and magazines for weeks. These experiences have given Charlotte a savvy wisdom that she shares as she talks candidly about careers, dating, fashion, sex, plastic surgery and that terrible demon of the twenty-first century – depression.

Funny and insightful, *Charlotte's Secrets* is crammed full of advice Charlotte wishes she had taken herself.